A MAN ON WOMEN

What do men really think about women in the twenty-first century?

WAYNE KEHL

PublishAmerica
Baltimore

First printing

PublishAmerica has allowed this work to remain exactly as the author intended, verbatim, without editorial input.

This publication contains the opinions and ideas of its author. Author intends to offer information of a general nature. Any reliance on the information herein is at the reader's own discretion.

Hardcover 978-1-4489-3749-3
Softcover 978-1-4489-3958-9
PUBLISHED BY PUBLISHAMERICA, LLLP
www.publishamerica.com
Baltimore

Printed in the United States of America

A MAN ON WOMEN

What do men really think about women in the twenty-first century?

ENTERTAINING

ENLIGHTENING

INFORMATIVE

BOLD

WARNING: THIS BOOK MIGHT CHANGE THE WAY
YOU THINK ABOUT WOMEN

DEDICATION

I dedicate this book to my mother, Muriel Helen Kehl.
Somewhere within the soul of every good man beats his
mother's heart...and that is the best part of him!

THE CHAPTERS

INTRODUCTION

As a fifty-something man who has worked with women most of his adult life, I have penned this book to bring some degree of clarity to the mysteries of man-woman relationships. I did not write this book because I think I know more about women than other men or because I have an astonishingly brilliant understanding of the minds of women... I wrote it because I am very much like the majority of men on the planet and therefore able to bring everyday thoughts of ordinary men to life on these pages. I am a behavioral analyst and journeyman manager of hundreds of people but this book is not about those things. This book is about what men are thinking about women while they are at work, at play and at rest. On these pages you will find my opinions, my observations and my interpretations of the actions and thoughts of all the women I have known in my life. The women I portray in this book are real, yet unidentified; they are the actual ladies who inspired me to write about them and as you will soon read, I will treat them with respect.

As a reasonably dominant person who has never been afraid to "mix it up" with other men when challenged in the business world or on the street, I often found myself drawn inexplicably to the softness and safety of the women in my life. I have always felt more comfortable with women and I dare say that I consider many of the women in my life much closer to me emotionally than the men I regularly associate with. I am willing to let my guard down with women and when I do that, I find they are willing to open up to me. With women, I need not be dominant in order to win a debate; with women, I need not become aggressive in order to exercise my right to an alternate opinion; with women I need not brag about my accomplishments in order to impress. With most women, when I am just myself, emotionally naked and unabashed, I can succeed in establishing a bond that can easily last a lifetime.

Women have loved me, saved me, carried me, and made me whole. They have brought me up when I was down and helped replace my scowl with a smile more times than I can remember. Men on the other hand have often turned my smile upside down and created anger where none had previously existed or benefited from its existence. Men have the need to dominate other men but conversely they have an ingrained, unfaltering need to care for and protect the women in their lives. What many men do not understand however, is that women do not necessarily want to be cared for and protected at all times. Often they want to win through singular effort and at all times, they want their thoughts to be heard. The greatest shock for many men will be that almost all women actually want to be in charge of something more than the kitchen and the household budget. Despite that, men should not be hated for acting naturally. They are the products of eons of male dominated cultural conditioning that has been diminished but not eliminated by evolution. The DNA strands of men are clogged with the primeval need to hunt and gather for their children and the women who bore them. That same DNA sometimes causes them to be less sensitive than women would like them to be.

Women are slowly taking their rightful place in society and that evolution confuses men. Their manly, male instincts tell them that women are on the planet for only one or two purposes…both of which are necessary, but neither of which is necessarily the thing that the ladies dream of doing as often as men would like. In this book you will find out why men are holding women back and why women are preventing themselves from moving forward. I truly hope that members of both genders are able to find a better understanding of why they feel the way they feel about the opposite sex. In this book, you will find humor along with thought provoking, controversial arguments. Mostly, you will find clarity and if I have accomplished what I set out to do, you will find a better understanding and appreciation for all of the male-female relationships in your life.

I hope you enjoy, "A MAN ON WOMEN".

Wayne Kehl

Women...
Who are they and where did they come from?

CHAPTER 1

Women in History

A s the men of the executive management committee of Maleo Industries strode into the oak-clad boardroom with its comfortable leather chairs and massive wood table, they knew they were in for a long day. It was September fifteenth, nineteen eighty-five, the day of the annual budget session and no one was looking forward to what was about to come. These meetings tended to drag on and during the management payroll section of the budget the discussions often became quite heated. Every vice president there had a strong view of the value of the managers who reported to him and each was ready to do battle to make sure his people were compensated fairly. In past years, as the meetings unfolded, a pattern hinting that fairness might be based in something other than ability or performance generally emerged.

Maleo's fifty seven year old president, Doug McCoy chaired his meetings with an iron fist. He was six feet five inches tall with a full head of well-groomed, poker-straight, silver hair. He was in great shape and quite muscular. Doug presented an imposing physical image at the head of the table. His Armani suit was perfectly pressed and the knot in his Nino Ceruti tie was so perfect that it looked as though Nino Ceruti had tied it himself. "All right, gentlemen, let's get on with this. I don't want to spend all day and all night in this room so I don't want to hear a lot of fluff about why your particular managers are better than someone else's. Just state your case and then I will decide if they deserve a raise or not! We will go through these from highest to lowest and knock 'em all off before lunch," he said in a loud, confident voice. "Got that?" Almost everyone at the table nodded obediently and grunted approval in unison…"Uh huh."

The only person who did not respond to McCoy was Wendy Taylor, his executive assistant who was there to take minutes. She sat at the opposite end of the table from her swarthy boss, head down, averting his gaze while staring blankly at the screen of her computer. Her fingers were poised, hovering over the keyboard awaiting his next words. Wendy did not enjoy these meeting because the words and actions of the executive men of Maleo indicated to her that either they were not aware that she was a woman, that they were not aware that she was present, or that none of them cared about her at all. She felt like a nameless, faceless, seemingly mindless ghost in the room and she hated the way that made her feel.

McCoy look directly at Bob Martin from the Eastern region saying, "Okay Bob, I see that you want to give that new guy Spencer Johnson another thousand bucks a month when he is already dragging down ninety five 'k' a year plus bonus? Is that realistic? I mean is he actually bringing that much value to us? You'd better tell me he is or I will have your ass, Bob! He is the highest paid branch manager we've got and as far as I'm concerned, we paid too much for him in the first place because you convinced me he's a hotshot!" McCoy said, glaring into the eyes of his Eastern vice president. Bob Martin laughed nervously before opening his lips to speak.

"Oh yah, Doug, Spencer is a great guy and his staff are rallying to support him. I see great things for him in the future," Bob stated softly, with a smattering of confidence.

"Give me numbers, Bob. I really don't give a damn about how much the staff like him. I want production and I want a return on investment. What has he done?" Bob asked with his chin in his palm and a furrow in his brow.

"Ummhhh, well I must admit that he has had a slow start, Doug. Sales production in his branch is up only one percent on a budget of five percent,

but I know he can pull it out. It is a big branch and the last manager left the place in pretty rough shape. Spencer is trying to play catch up now," Bob blurted.

Doug McCoy, lifted his chin from his palm, sat up straight and looked Bob Martin straight in the eye. "Don't con me, Bob! Can this guy do it or not?"

"I'm dead certain he can! I will bet my reputation on it!" Bob replied with an air of confidence.

"Okay, he's got the raise! All I wanted was some buy-in from you, Bob. After all these years, you should know that," Doug McCoy said with a hint of disgust. "How about you, Smithson? What the hell are you trying to do, giving that little wimp Chris Dickson another fifteen hundred when he is already making ninety 'k'? At that rate he will be making more than Bob's prima donna!"

Alex Smithson was much tougher than Bob Martin and he came prepared. "Boss, his branch profit is already eight hundred thousand over budget year to date, which is a fifteen percent lift and he is on track to be over by slightly more than a million at year end. He is doing an amazing job." Alex looked up from his spreadsheets and smiled arrogantly at Bob Martin before turning back to Doug McCoy.

"Well, I guess there is not much I can say about that is there, Al? Okay give the little wimp his raise and tell him if he doesn't make the million, I will personally throw his butt out onto the street!" McCoy challenged with a laugh.

The day progressed as usual…each vice president taking body blows of criticism and derision from Doug McCoy when their turn came around. It all went as expected with few surprises until they got to the vice president of operations for the Southern region, Max McMaster. "Okay, Max I am looking at this payroll sheet and I am seeing a manager by the name of Debbie Wilson who is already making fifty thousand a year and you want to pay her an additional seven hundred and fifty bucks a month. Are you nuts?" McCoy asked with genuine shock and dismay in his voice.

Max McMaster's mother had raised him alone after his father was killed in an automobile accident when Max was six years old. He was an only child and his close relationship with mother created in him a deep and abiding respect for women. He believed that women had as much value in the workplace as men and throughout his working career he had striven for workplace equality. When Doug McCoy challenged him on Debbie's raise Max was ready. "Doug, her branch generates more revenue than Chris Dickson's and her bottom line is up eighteen percent, year to date. She is on track for a lift of a million and half before year end and frankly, without her we would be screwed!" Max stated passionately and loudly. He expected an argument and he got.

"Oh for Christ's sake Max, stop being such a bleeding heart liberal and get real! She is a woman and you have managed to drive her salary up over the years well beyond what we pay any other woman in our organization. It just doesn't look good! How the hell are we going to explain this to all of the other skirts in the company? Answer me that!" Doug screamed.

"I don't have to answer that, Doug. It is a stupid question! She is a better manager than anyone else we have in this company and you know it! Some day you will realize that you can't keep paying women less than they're worth while you treat them like second-class citizens!" Max retorted, his top lip quivering with raw emotion. Too overwrought to speak anymore, he slumped back in his chair staring into Doug McCoy's eyes awaiting the inevitable return volley. He only had to wait a couple of seconds...

"Well it won't be today, McMaster!" McCoy hollered, referring to Max's earlier statement. "I will not give that woman another red cent during this decade. She is overpaid for a woman and I am sick of your silly attitude. God, if I didn't know better I would think you're sleeping with her!"

With that, Wendy Taylor who had been sitting listening silently, wiped away a tear as it ran down her cheek. Doug McCoy seeing her obvious display of emotion, shouted, "My God, Wendy, pull yourself together...you've heard worse than that before!" His outburst was more

24

than Wendy could take. Saying nothing, she pushed her chair back and ran from the room weeping. As she slammed the heavy boardroom door behind her, Max jumped up to follow her out.

"You really did it this time, Doug! God, you are such a heartless maniac!" Max yelled as he backed through the door, on his way to comfort Wendy.

Doug, slightly embarrassed but more than a little proud of himself, sensed the tension in the room. He scanned the faces of the remaining vice presidents defiantly in order to prove his dominance. No one blinked and no one spoke as he made eye contact with each and every one of them. When he was certain he had their attention, Doug McCoy said quietly but matter-of-factly, "They'll be back. Let's get this show on the road."

Scenes similar to this played out in the boardrooms of North America during most decades of the late twentieth century. Women have had a long, uphill climb toward equality and although they are nearer the top, the incline is steeper than ever. In years past, Doug McCoy was a typical company president and his attitude toward women in the workplace was unfortunately and sadly, very common. Now that we have had a taste of a boardroom in the nineteen eighties, let's take a walk through history to review what some famous, successful women have done to rise above the oppression of our male dominated society and gain notoriety in a man's world.

****

Women…who are they and where did they come from? Of course, with an opener like that, I could immediately launch into a well-researched thesis on creation and the evolution of man and womankind…or perhaps even a theoretical, religious discussion of Adam and Eve in the Garden of Eden. However, as you might have guessed, my question is purely rhetorical.

What I want to discover is how women got to the point they are at right now, during this space in time. Why are women the way they are; why are they what they are; and who lead them to their current status of being and existence in the world.

Cave drawings from prehistoric times show men hunting and gathering, while women cooked and looked after the children. Evolving women didn't stand a chance! Even cavemen thought women were more useful in the kitchen and the nursery than out in the world earning a living. If you live in North America, you are probably familiar with the all too common depiction of a caveman dragging his woman around by her hair. That bit of insulting artwork has adorned many a comic strip and humorous literary work over the past few decades. The image of a powerful male vanquishing his subservient female speaks volumes about the position of ownership and dominance that men have taken in society. Note that I have used the word *"his"* in reference to the woman. *His woman* or *my woman, are* terms I still hear used today when men refer to their wives and girlfriends. Both terms tend to diminish the value of women and force their gender into a position similar to that of a commodity that has been purchased or simply taken by a man. Of course we all wince a little when we hear that terminology, but we are okay with the terms, *his wife* or *my wife.* Why are those terms acceptable? Why is it okay to use a term of ownership for a wife but not for a woman? After all, a wife is most often a woman and a woman is very often a wife. How about, *his old lady* or *my old lady?* How do you feel when you hear those terms? I become embarrassed and uncomfortable when I hear one of my fellow men using that terminology in public…or even in private. In actual practice, those terms are generally not used correctly since it is seldom that an old man will actually call his wife an *old lady.* This is perplexing since most old men are married to old ladies but I usually find young men calling their young wives, *old ladies*. That makes no sense at all in a literal way. It is clear that men, who use terms such as *my woman* or *his old lady*, wish to subjugate and oppress any woman who chooses to become a spouse to a man. Again, I find that perplexing because I do not believe that oppression can possibly be a strong foundation for a loving relationship. And besides that, why would anyone want to be married to someone who would rather oppress than honor her or him?

At this point, I am imagining that the women reading this are thinking, "Yah...right on!" while the men are saying, "Jeez, we can't get away with anything anymore!"

It is clear that when using negative terminology, men are unconsciously trying to boost their own stature and prove their dominance over the women in their lives. They are flexing their relationship muscles in a subtle, and in their minds, humorous way. They often mean no harm at all and cannot understand why women react so strongly to words that are essentially harmless when allowed to stand on their own. Modern man is the product of his environment and he has a lifetime of peer pressure and cultural imprinting to cheer him on. We men are fallible and often insensitive creatures. I like to think though, that most of us make up for it in other ways.

Unfortunately negative, oppressive language pervades our male dominated society to the point that it has become almost acceptable. Because I want a *"G"* rating on this book, I will not use the common curse words that men use against women. Most men and women already have a good grasp of the meanings, spellings and pronunciations of the majority of North American curse words so there is no need for me to repeat them here. The list is long and their intent is generally to be demeaning and harmful. You are probably leafing through your mental volumes of curse words as you are reading this right now. Interestingly, as

I mentally leaf through my volumes, I am able to come up with more curse words associated with women than with men. Modern media has exacerbated the situation by using negative cursing language commonly in publications, broadcasts, and telecasts that are available to adults and children of all ages. I make no value judgments on the freedom of the press, other than to say that rightly or wrongly, a culture is created by continued, broad based exposure to ideas, values, and compelling events. Our North American media has the power to shape and control the thoughts, wishes and dreams of its audience as it sees fit. Over the course of the last century they have used their power for good and for evil depending on their target audience and the wills of their producers and sponsors. On a positive note, I believe the media has *raised* the stature of women as much as they have torn it down. Thanks to those purveyors of news, sports, and gossip I believe the cause of women's liberation is winning out over the cause of male dominance in the twenty first century. We must be careful though because there can be no real winners in a public fight between men and women. If women win, men lose. If men win, women lose. Either way, life will be unpleasant for *both* genders. My hope is that we will reach a mutually agreeable balance and true equality at some time in the near future. Equality can really only be achieved when both sides agree that they are equal…and therein lies the rub!

Moving back to history, let's talk about how women have evolved since Neanderthal days. The Neanderthals were really very poor historians and biographers so we will have to fast forward to less ancient history. Despite male dominance, numerous powerful queens have graced the pages of history over the centuries. **Cleopatra,** (69 BC to 30 BC) the most famous queen or Pharaoh of Egypt, had incredible power that was God-given and irrevocable during her rein. Not unlike the culture of

Hollywood, ancient Egypt allowed female children of powerful people to become powerful unto themselves. Cleopatra's father was Ptolemy XII, descendent of Alexander's General so you know that she had a great start in life from a patriarchal perspective. Unfortunately, despite her great power, Cleopatra contributed to man's subjugation of women when she committed suicide by snakebite after her lover Marc Antony took his own life. She chose not to carry on after the man who stole her heart also broke it, shattering her spirit. As strong and powerful as she was, she could not bear to spend another minute on earth without her man. One of the greatest blows to womankind at that time in history was that after her death, Egypt was taken over by Octavian Caesar thereby putting the country back into the hands of a man…and a foreign man at that!

Nefertiti, the famed *Sun Queen* of Egypt (1330 BC to 1370 BC) of the 18th Dynasty was touted as one of the most beautiful and powerful female rulers of all time. I am not sure who her parents were, but her husband was Akhenaton aka Amenhotep IV. Akhenaton created a divine trinity with sun God Aken, Nefertiti, and himself as the leaders of a powerful cult. He was able to use the divinity of the sun God to enhance the power of the king, which gave his beautiful wife Nefertiti and himself more power than any other rulers of the era. The literal translation of the word Nefertiti is *"a beautiful woman has come."* Imagine the power that a woman of that stature must have had. She was admired and adored by all who knew of her. She lived a life of luxury and fame and was a bit of a feminist herself. Nefertiti was the first known queen of Egypt to be seen in public wearing the same Nubian wig as her husband. She was also known to rule alongside her husband Akhenaton with equal power. In fact, her power was so absolute that she is pictured in reliefs of the era twice as often as Akhenaton, the King.

Unfortunately, it seems that Nefertiti disappeared mysteriously after the death of her daughter, Mekataten. It is not known if she was banished or died from a plague. Alternatively it is fabled that she might have come back to rule until she turned the throne over to her son in law, Tutankhamen. In any case, what we do know is that she left behind a legacy as one of the most powerful leaders of all time. As feminine and beautiful as she was, she chose to move beyond typical female objectivity to a life of power and fame. In her own way, Nefertiti was a model for all women in the twenty-first century.

Moving into more modern times, let's consider one of the most well known women in recorded history. **Joan of Arc**, (Jeanne d'Arc or Jeanne la Pucelle) was born near Burgundy in France on January 6, 1412. When Joan was thirteen, she began hearing voices telling her it was her duty to save France from England. The throne of France had been claimed by the English royalty due to the repatriation of an inheritance created by the intermingling of the genes of various French and English monarchs. As you might expect, that was a very unpopular and controversial decision in the minds and hearts of the citizens of France. In 1429 Joan managed to persuade a local baron to send her to the castle of the true French King, Charles VII where she convinced the dauphin or heir to the throne to allow her to lead the French army to the city of Orleans, which was under siege by the English. Her army was victorious in that battle and many others, ultimately bringing Charles VII to the royal court at Rheims to be crowned as the official King of France. Joan was given a place of honor next to the King during the coronation ceremony. When Joan attempted to recapture Paris from the English in 1430, she failed and was later captured in battle, sold to the English, and tried in a court of law as a sorceress and heretic. Even though Charles VII, whom she had repatriated as

King could have saved her by paying off her captors, he refused and she was burned at the stake on May 30, 1431. King Charles, perhaps having a stroke of guilt, had her condemnation as a heretic annulled in 1456 and she now rests as a French national heroine, admired the world over. Even though she was only nineteen years old when she died, Joan of Arc had an illustrious military career and was even canonized by Pope Benedict XV in May of 1920. Here is why Joan of Arc is so well suited for a mention in this book: Interestingly, despite her incredible success in battle, Joan was severely chastised for her habit of wearing men's clothing. The Bishop of Beauvais actually considered the fact that she wore men's clothing as a crime against God. As the legend goes, that charge and her refusal to change out of her male garb, led to the charge of sorcery and heresy against her…and ultimately to her execution. As you can see, Joan of Arc was a feminist of the highest order and ultimately gave her life for the right to be herself. Despite her great deeds, the male rulers of her era were unwilling to accept her as she was, and ultimately killed her because of her beliefs. Her courage and resolute determination should be honored and emulated by all members of both genders today.

You have probably heard of the *Elizabeth Fry Society*…but who was **Elizabeth Fry**? Born on May 21, 1780 Elizabeth Gurney was the daughter of a prominent banker and businessman in Norwich, England. At an early age Elizabeth felt the need to help those less fortunate and could often be found gathering clothing for the poor, visiting the sick, and teaching poor children to read. She married a Quaker, Joseph Fry on August 18, 1800. Between 1800 and 1817, Elizabeth gave birth to eleven children and in 1811 became a preacher with the Society of Friends. At the urging of a family friend, she visited Newgate prison to find over 300 women and their children crammed together in two large cells. The women were forced to wash, cook and sleep in the cells night and day. They slept on the floor with no bedding of any kind. Feeling overwhelming compassion, Elizabeth began visiting the women of Newgate Prison on a regular basis, bringing clothing and setting up a school for them. Eventually, she began working with prison officials to create a system of compulsory sewing duties and bible readings. In 1817 she formed the *Association for the Improvement of the Female Prisoners in Newgate.* Elizabeth's brother in law, Thomas Fowell Buxton a British MP, decided to bring her work to the attention of the House of Commons. She testified before the House giving information on the deplorable and inhumane state of British prisons. Although the majority of the Members of Parliament agreed with much of what Elizabeth espoused, they became quite annoyed when she stated, *"Capital punishment is evil and produces evil results."* In those days in Great Britain there were over 200 offences, including stealing of clothes and forging banknotes, which were punishable by death. Sure enough, in February of 1817, two women were sentenced to death for forgery. Elizabeth Fry campaigned for their reprieve, but was unsuccessful. She was branded a dangerous reformer who was attempting to eliminate the dread of punishment amongst the criminal classes. However, Elizabeth's hard work paid off when the 1823 Gaols act was passed and many of her recommended prison reforms were put into place. She became a celebrity in Britain and was attacked in the press for her success with the male-controlled Government and prison systems. Her good work could not be denied but they criticized her for neglecting her family while pursuing her causes. In 1828 Elizabeth's husband Joseph went bankrupt and although she had nothing to do with his business dealings, her reputation suffered as a result. Despite that setback, Elizabeth and Joseph forged on with their charity work and reform for workplaces, prisons, and hospitals. Queen Victoria took notice of Elizabeth's work and after meeting with her several times provided funding for some of her good works. The Queen once wrote that Elizabeth Fry was a *very superior person.* She died after a short illness on October 12, 1845. Despite the fact that her Quaker religion did not allow for a funeral service, over a thousand people attended her burial. Elizabeth Fry was a person of influence with the courage of a thousand soldiers and the heart of a lion. Although not a feminist, she is proof that a woman *can* make a positive difference in a male dominated world.

While Elizabeth Fry was making a difference in England, **Susan B. Anthony** was growing up on the other side of the pond. Born in Adams, Massachusetts on February 15, 1820, Susan B. Anthony, like Elizabeth Fry, was a Quaker. She was also a teacher and one of the earliest, true women's rights leaders. She campaigned for women's suffrage and even took the controversial stand of stating that black men should not be given the right to vote in United States elections before women. She was ridiculed in newspapers and was the victim of satirical cartoons. Despite numerous, deeply personal attacks, she carried on fighting for the vote for women, giving speeches all across the country and even suffering arrest and conviction in 1872 for attempting to cast a ballot in Rochester, New York. Susan B. Anthony was largely responsible for women gaining the right to vote but never saw the ultimate fruits of her labor. She died on March 13, 1906. Women were given the right to vote when the Nineteenth Amendment to the Constitution was passed fourteen years after her death. Susan B. Anthony was instrumental in allowing women to vote...perhaps the most important stepping-stone of the women's movement in history. She paved the way for strong women after her to take their rightful place in society. Women everywhere should be very proud of, and thankful to this early feminist.

Mother Teresa was born Agnes Gonxha Bojaxhiu in Skopje, Macedonia on August 26 in the year 1910. She lived until September 5, 1997 and as one of the most recognized and revered women in the world, she had an amazing career. Her father died when she was eight years old and her mother Dranafile Bojaxhiu raised her as a Catholic. Fascinated by stories of the lives of missionaries, by age 12 she had already decided to dedicate her life to religion and to helping those less fortunate. At the age of eighteen she left home and joined the Sisters of Loreto in Dublin, Ireland. After only a short period of training, she was sent to India where in May of 1931 she took her vows as a nun and began teaching at St. Mary's High School in Calcutta. At that time she chose the name Teresa. In 1948, feeling extreme compassion for the poor and hungry of India, she received permission from her order to leave her teaching job and work amongst the poor in the slums of Calcutta. In October of 1950 she received permission to start her own order, *The Missionaries of Charity*. Mother Teresa's order devoted itself to assistance and care for those the world had forgotten. In 1979, the order was expanded to include *The Contemplative Branch of the Brothers* and in 1984 a Priest branch was created. Today, her order has spread all over the world and it continues to assist the world's poorest people. In addition to that, they take on relief work after natural disasters and epidemics. In North America, Europe and Australia they also take care of shut-ins, alcoholics, the homeless and the sick. She has had commemorations named for her, and numerous churches, buildings and even roads have been named after her. Various politicians, pundits and journalists criticized her despite her good work, for bringing negative views of India to the world, and for forcing her Catholic views upon Indian

Nationals. Despite that criticism, she forged on and was generally regarded as selfless, energetic and courageous in her work with the poor. Because of her good work, she was granted an Indian state funeral and was allowed to lie in state in St. Thomas, Kolkata for one week prior to her funeral. It is amazing to me that a little girl from Macedonia could create a worldwide movement while working tirelessly with the poor and sick in the streets of India. There is a certain power that some human beings possess that makes them superior to common mortals. Driven by her overwhelming desire to be of service to others, Mother Teresa was one of those superior people. If every woman on earth carried the power of Mother Teresa, the feminine side of humanity would surely rule the world without challenge from any man.

Rosa Parks was a modern day heroin in every sense of the word. She was born Rosa Louise McCauley in Tuskegee, Alabama on February 4, 1913 the daughter of a carpenter and a schoolteacher. At the age of 11 she enrolled in the Montgomery Industrial School for girls. It was a private school, paid for by wealthy Northern women that taught self-reliance and self worth for young women. During her childhood she was witness to the sights and sounds of Ku Klux Klan lynching's and beatings. She admitted freely that she grew up in an environment of fear that ultimately made her fearless. On December 1, 1955 Rosa did the unthinkable! In Montgomery, Alabama the segregation laws of the day indicated that when riding buses, African Americans had to pay the bus driver at the front of the bus and then leave the bus and walk to the rear of it to enter through the back door. Black people could only sit in designated seats at the rear of the bus and if the bus became too full, they would be required to vacate their seats in order to allow white people to be seated. The displaced Black people would have to move even farther back or stand up during the ride. Interestingly two thirds of the bus riders in Montgomery at that time in history were African Americans. On the day in question, Rosa got on the bus and sat in the last seat available. It was at the back of the bus and well behind the white riders. As the bus made more stops, more white people entered. Because the bus was completely full, one of the white men was forced to stand with no seat available to him. When the driver saw him standing, he ordered four African American riders in Rosa's row to vacate their seats so the white rider could sit down. In those days it was also unacceptable for black people and white people to sit across from each other or in the same row. Three of the black people stood up but Rosa did not. The driver told her that if she did not move, he would call the police. She told him that he may call the police and she was subsequently arrested. Later that week her bail was posted by a lawyer she knew and Rosa's arrest soon became the greatest test case ever for activists in the African American community. The Women's Political Council printed up 35,000 handbills urging African Americans to boycott the Montgomery city bus system. Backed by the famous Reverend Dr. Martin Luther King, the boycott and protest worked well, as most Black people in the community stayed off the buses for over a year. Rosa's trial lasted only thirty minutes and she was found guilty. Led by Dr. Martin Luther King the civil rights movement in the United States became front-page news and Dr. King was acknowledged as its leader. On December 21, 1956 the United States Supreme Court ruled that segregation on public transit was illegal. Despite that social victory, Rosa and her family were harassed and threatened until they finally moved to Detroit, Michigan in 1957. She worked there for U.S. Representative John Conyers, Democrat Michigan. Rosa also founded the Rosa and Raymond Parks institute for Self Development, to aid young people. In 1999 President Clinton awarded her with a Congressional Gold Medal. She never stopped fighting against racial injustice until her death in 2005 at the age of 92. She was the first American woman ever to lie in state at the Nation's Capitol...that honor was usually reserved for U.S. Presidents. It goes without saying that Rosa Parks was an amazing human being and an outstanding example of womankind.

In modern times, women are making great strides in the fields of entertainment and politics. In the area of television and radio, female talk show hosts have become virtual heroines to the world due to incredible acts of altruism and exposure of important social issues. The talk show ladies have become modern day suffragettes, revered by all. A number of other women have come into the spotlight and under the microscope by moving into politics at the highest level. I am willing to speculate that the United States will have a female President before the end of the twenty first century. The first female president will owe a number of courageous, prominent ladies of the past a huge debt and characteristically, I expect she will acknowledge them with a genuine display of gratitude.

And, so ends the history lesson. The reason that I have provided all of this information is to point out that despite their obvious physical differences, there have been many women on earth since time began who were capable of rising above their femininity...those who attempted to break out of the mold and emancipate women from the bonds of the male dominated world. Many have been successful and yet, their accomplishments have been considered as exceptions or *one-offs*. It is almost as if when a woman has done something great, she must be considered privileged; unusual; pushy; difficult; a freak of her gender; or someone who should be resented by men and made the brunt of disgusting humor by them. Every one of the women I mentioned has had detractors and has suffered much criticism for her efforts. Every one of them rose up and pushed passed her detractors to claim her rightful place in history. They proved that the female stereotype is neither valid nor necessary.

Men appear to have ruled the world through sheer muscular strength and brute force that is produced by an overabundance of testosterone...that chemical that makes men hairier than women; that element that gives men more muscle mass than women; that thing that makes men more aggressive than women. Powerful stuff! Testosterone does not create brain mass or enhance intelligence however. That fact alone might just be the single element that will allow women to make greater strides than men in the twenty first century.

It is clear that today we live in a kinder, softer world where big muscles, aggressive tendencies and body hair are not elemental to success. In politics, finances, business and entertainment women are catching up with men and may soon overtake them. Women are also finding success in police departments, construction companies, and retail management. They are leading large companies, manufacturing all sorts of consumer goods, and producing television shows.

So why are most businesses and industries still controlled by men? Why are there still comparatively few women gaining popularity or even, notoriety as Captains of industry? Read on...

I'm not in the mood…
But I don't know why!

CHAPTER 2
Women and Hormones

By the time Max McMaster returned to the boardroom, the payroll review was finished and the group had moved on to sales production targets. That discussion would prove to be equally as heated as the last one, but fortunately for Max, Maleo Industries had never even dreamed of putting a woman into outside sales, so only men would be on the hot plate for the next while. He would not be quite so compelled to lose his composure as he had during the last encounter.

Max cracked the door open and slipped in as quietly as possible. He was attempting not to be noticed as he returned to his place at the executive table…but he would not be so lucky.

"So you finally came back!" Doug McCoy snapped. "You missed most of the compensation review so I had to make some tough decisions on your behalf…and you probably won't like them. That's what happens when you walk out on me!"

As much as Max was furious with his boss and wanted to do battle with him, he needed his job and chose to remain silent. He simply looked blankly at McCoy, hoping that he would move on to the next subject.

"So where the hell is Wendy?" Doug asked, looking directly at Max.

"She got in her car and drove away, Doug. I think she's going home," Max said quietly.

"Oh for God's sake! It must be her time of the month. That's the problem with women...if it's not one thing it's the other with them!" Doug mumbled. Turning to Max again Doug raised his voice and said, "And that my soft-hearted friend is why women will never get ahead in business! Get used to it!"

Max said nothing, choosing to allow the meeting to move on to more productive things.

Hormonal issues and monthly cycles have been the root cause of the devaluation of women in the work world for centuries. Let's see if all of the hype is true...

****

In the course of researching material for this book, I learned a lot about the physiological makeup of women. I also learned that medical science is far from certain about how female hormones affect the minds of women, (if at all) and that although female hormones are quite different than male hormones, they are often incorrectly blamed for negative behavior, moodiness, and loss of sex drive.

Male and female hormones are known as estrogens and androgens respectively. Interestingly, both types of hormones, male and female, are present in both genders. It might come as quite a shock to some of the burly guys down at the gym that they are packing around female hormones in their big, hairy bodies but really, it is quite normal. Don't worry guys; most of you have far more male hormones than female ones!

Hormones can be defined as chemical substances produced by an endocrine gland that has an effect on the functions of certain organs in the body. Most men produce 6 to 8 milligrams of the male hormone, testosterone, (an androgen) per day while most women produce only 0.5 milligrams of testosterone daily.

Conversely, women produce far more estrogens than men but men do produce small amounts of those as well. Estrogens are generally considered to be sex hormones and are produced primarily in a female's ovaries. They cause the growth of female sex organs, breasts, and pubic hair while regulating menstrual cycles. In addition, estrogens are important in maintaining the elasticity and lubrication of the vaginal lining along with preserving the texture and function of female breasts. My goodness, women are so complicated!

Although present in men in small quantities, estrogens are not responsible for any known male function. However, if there happens to be an unusually high level of estrogens present in a man, they may suffer from reduced sex drive, erectile dysfunction, possible breast enlargement, and loss of body hair. Androgens (testosterone being the primary one) are manufactured in large quantity by the male testes, but are produced in smaller quantities in female ovaries. It is also produced by the adrenal glands of both sexes. Androgens cause the development of the testes and penis in male babies. They cause puberty to occur and they influence the development of facial hair, body hair and pubic hair. They also typically cause the deepening of the voice along with muscle development in pubescent boys. Androgens are essentially what make men different from women. So you see, Ladies men are quite complicated too!

Testosterone is a primary driver of sexual desire in both genders. Although women carry much less testosterone than men, they are able to detect much lower levels of it in their bloodstreams which allows them to have just as much sex drive as men. Men on the other hand, will often suffer from reduced sex drive if a physiological problem exists that prevents normal testosterone production. Although women will suffer from

reduced estrogen production after menopause, their sex drive seldom abates because the loss of estrogen causes only minor physiological changes to their sex organs such as loss of elasticity and decreased vaginal lubrication. Sometimes they can eliminate those problems through doctor prescribed hormone replacement therapy. It is apparent from all of this that men are more likely to lose sex drive than women when testosterone production reduces due to age or some physiological challenge. That leads me to the conclusion that when women are *not in the mood* for sex, their lack of desire is not hormonally driven but is instead, the result of some other problem. It is also believed that sexual appetite is more influenced by the senses of sight, smell, hearing and touch than it is by hormones. In other words, people are more likely to become aroused by overt sexual stimulation than because of their own hormones. By the way, there are no hard and fast rules on sex drive. Abnormally low levels of testosterone in men and women sometimes have no affect whatsoever on sexual appetite and should not be blamed for an unhappy sex life until the problem has been investigated by a qualified medical professional.

On the moodiness front, there has been some medical study done on the concept that fluctuations in female sex hormones can actually cause changes in the responsiveness of the female brain. There is a belief that women's brains are more responsive and therefore their attitudes may be more open and accepting if they are in a pre-menstrual phase prior to ovulation than they are during the post ovulation phase. In other words because they have a high level of estrogen and progesterone in their bodies prior to ovulation they are more likely to be in a good mood then than after ovulation. That happens because most women are producing eggs much of the time during most months. When sperm from a male is not present in the womb or sperm is not able

to fertilize a mature egg, the levels of estrogen and progesterone in the female body begin to fall and when that happens, her mood might change as a result of the hormonal fluctuation. At the same time, without the support of those vital female hormones, the lining of the womb is shed. Once that happens, the female is able to begin producing more eggs to start the reproduction process all over again. This is commonly known as the monthly period or menstrual cycle.

It is generally accepted by medical science that there is no true clinical understanding of the relationship of female cycles to depression or stress disorders. There appears to be growing evidence however, that estrogen hormones may play a critical role in mood disorders of women. Since men seldom have fluctuations in their hormone levels and have no monthly menstrual cycle they are less likely to have hormone related mood swings. I should point out that I am not a doctor but everything I have written here is a compilation of research done by various reputable universities and medical professionals. I draw no scientific conclusions and have no intention of appearing to be an expert in the field. I am however confident that this information is accurate and extremely valuable to the study of human behavior.

So there you have it...a clinical discussion of *femaleness*. Because of the miracle of creation and the need for repopulation of the planet, men and women are dramatically different on a physiological level. So what does the average man think about all of this? Not much! Most men do not really understand hormones or menstrual cycles. Most men are quite uncomfortable when forced into a discussion on these matters and most would rather not know anything at all about the inner workings of their mate. All they really want to know is that they have a great relationship with someone they find sexually appealing and mentally stimulating. If you try to talk to them about the monthly cycle of their beautiful, sexy, intelligent wife, they will run for the hills!

Women need to understand that most men are uncomfortable talking about periods and cycles. They must understand that most men feel a sense of detachment from the clinical elements of the miracle of creation and even when speaking of childbirth, they really just want to talk about the baby…not the birth. I suppose there is a percentage of the male population who thoroughly enjoy seeing their mate giving birth and talking about the placenta or episiotomy afterwards, but most of us just want a baby to nurture and teach how to ride a bike. All of that birthing stuff is the domain of the fairer sex and they can have it all to themselves. There are not many men (but amazingly there have been some) who would want the opportunity to actually carry a baby for nine months and then give birth, legs wide open, in front of their spouse and a host of medical professionals. It appears that those 6 to 8 milligrams of testosterone that we men are producing everyday prevent us from coming to grips with the most elemental functions of procreation. In addition to the fact that men do not generally have an adequate level of pain tolerance to handle childbirth, we are squeamish about those things…and we are sorry about that! If women want to get along with men a little better, they should consider the tolerance level of the men in their lives to menstrual cycles, gory birth stories, and *female problems*.

Female estrogens are also responsible for the development of fat in certain areas of every woman's body. Interestingly, those deposits play a big part in male/female relationships. During puberty, hormones naturally cause the development of fat deposits in the areas of the female breasts, hips, buttocks, and thighs. The small amount of testosterone that women have in their system causes the necessary promotion of muscle and bone growth to support their growing bodies. Because women have less testosterone than estrogen, the weight distribution that occurs during puberty typically leans toward a more curvy *hourglass* shape as opposed to the *not-so-curvy*, thinner, more muscular shape that teenage boys generally develop. That explains why women have much more difficulty developing the kind of muscle tissue that would allow them to have the physical strength of men. You see, women are the *weaker sex* through no fault of their own. Their physiology is designed more for child bearing than hunting and gathering. They simply do not normally have the physiological capability to be as strong or as large as men. Those exceptional women who manage to develop large, manly muscles often have trouble attracting a male mate. No man wants to date a woman with bigger biceps than his own!

It is a commonly accepted myth that men think about sex every seven seconds. Disappointingly, that fable, although glorious for the guys, is probably not accurate. Unfortunately after much debate amongst various psychologists and sex experts about the frequency of male sexual fantasizing, the seven-second rule has been generally discarded as a wish rather than a fact. However, it is fair to say that men think about sex very often. But what are they specifically thinking about? They are thinking about how virtually any woman in their field of view would look naked, how attractive various components of any woman's body are, and what sex would be like with virtually any woman they come into contact with. They are thinking about actual past sexual encounters, pornography, or even a weather girl they saw on television the night before. Men have an incredible propensity for generating sexually charged visualizations in their minds. The large level of testosterone in their bodies drives their thoughts, almost involuntarily, to sex on a regular and frequent basis. I am sorry, Ladies but even the most genteel and well-spoken men in your lives are probably thinking about sex when they are talking to you about the speed of your hard drive, the price of gasoline, or the aroma of a cooking turkey. They can't help themselves. Socially aware, more evolved gentlemen however, will control their natural urges and conduct themselves in a respectful manner at all times. Despite physiology, men in the twenty first century have no right to force their hormone-driven thoughts or desires upon females, (or males) who have no desire to be party to them. We are not cavemen anymore and you don't have to put up with it, Ladies!

Many men are often quite particular about the types of female bodies they prefer. You have probably heard about *leg-men, breast-men, butt-men,* and even a few *face or hair-men.* The reasons for selection of a particular body part as a favorite is lost on me, but I do know why the various female body parts draw men to women for sex. On an evolutionary basis, human beings evolved from amoebas to the most intelligent and powerful creatures on earth due to superior intelligence and reproductive prowess. It is that reproductive instinct that causes men to be attracted to women. Large breasts, large hips, narrow waists, and protruding posteriors on women are all indications of a natural ability to reproduce, bear children, and nurture babies. Men don't actually think about reproduction when they are ogling women, but that is the primitive instinct that drives their thoughts about sex. Even the amount of redness in a woman's lips and cheeks has sexual overtones since lips and cheeks have a tendency to become engorged with blood during orgasm. When a woman appears to be ready to orgasm, it indicates that she is also ready to have sex and therefore ready to become pregnant and ultimately to bear children. Because of these fundamental reproductive instincts, women in the twenty first century continue to exaggerate the redness of their lips and cheeks with cosmetics, wear body-enhancing undergarments, and undergo significant and even dangerous surgeries to make themselves appear more capable of reproduction. Women and men believe all of those procedures and cosmetics are intended only to make them more beautiful or sexy for their partner...or so that they can attract a mate. In reality, the behavior actually stems from the basic, primeval and evolutionary need to reproduce and repopulate the planet with human beings. Women want to reproduce too, so they deliberately enhance their appearance in order to attract men and their sperm. They may not be thinking outwardly about reproduction, but that is the driving force behind their beautification efforts. Please don't allow this information to take the fun out of sex for you. Because we are human we are able to take the technical elements out of sexual reproduction and turn them into recreation, fantasy, and fun. We are one of very few animals on earth that practice sex for pleasure. Taken one step further, unlike other warm blooded animals, we are able to move sexual reproduction beyond a natural need for survival to one of the most enjoyable, fundamental and integral elements of any loving relationship.

This discussion of hormones, reproduction, and human attraction has provided some inkling as to why men and women are the way they are. It is however, just the beginning...

CHAPTER 3
Women at Work

It was nineteen ninety one, almost six years after the budget session that sent Wendy Taylor storming out of the boardroom in tears, and another budget session had come around at Maleo Industries. This time it was different. The cast of executives had changed.

"Hey guys, where's Doug McCoy today?" Max McMaster asked naively.

Alex Smithson looked at Max with a smile and asked, "You've been on holidays for a month or so haven't you, Max?"

"Yup! I had a great holiday with my family in Hawaii," Max said gleefully.

"Well, while you were basking in the sun, the mighty Doug McCoy was being fired!" Alex said, almost nervously. The room went silent; no one dared speak.

"Jeez, how could that happen?" Max asked with obvious shock in his voice. "What did he do?"

"I gather it was a combination of things. You know how he always like to mouth off about women and how they would never get anywhere in the business world?" Alex asked.

"Yahhh…" Max answered with anticipation.

Alex pondered what he was about to say for a moment before speaking again. "Well, unbeknownst to any of us, Doug had been hitting on Wendy

Taylor for years. Apparently he was into some pretty kinky stuff and when he put his cards on the table and invited her to join him in some sort of sexual adventure with another woman, she blew the whistle on him. I hear that she had been quietly patient for years and just put his advances off to childish, bad behavior. He went too far this time though and when he made a definite and clear offer of sexual activity, it scared her and she decided to turn him in to the board of directors. Weird stuff huh?"

"Weird is right!" Max said. "That explains why Wendy was so upset when Doug got mad at her during that board meeting in eighty five. He really was a piece of work! So tell me more…how did it go down? I want details!"

"It was just like I said. Apparently she called Hugh Braxton, the chairman of the board at home the same night that Doug came on to her. The next day, Hugh came into the office and had a private meeting in the boardroom with her. Then he called in a couple of the other women in the office…I think they were brought in to confirm Wendy's story. The next thing you know, Doug went into the boardroom for the last time. It was over in minutes. He stomped out of the boardroom straight into his office and started packing his stuff into a cardboard box. If you go into his office right now you will find a lot of his personal things still in there but I don't think he is coming back for them. He marched out of here like his life depended on it. He didn't talk to anyone; didn't make eye contact; didn't look back. He's just gone!" Bill said with a note of alarm in his voice.

"So how is Wendy now?" Max asked with genuine concern.

"I don't know. I haven't seen her since. Maybe she is taking some time off, or maybe they transferred her to another office…" Alex was about to say more but he was interrupted.

"I know where she is," Bob Martin answered knowingly. He had been listening to the two men from the end of the table.

"Well! Where is she?" Max demanded impatiently.

"She quit. She lasted about four days after McCoy got the axe, but between the harassment from the sales guys and even some of the women in

the office, the embarrassment and stress just got to her," Bob said sympathetically.

"Have you heard from her, Bob?" Max asked calmly.

"Yah, she called me from home the day she decided to quit. She told me that the whole ordeal had been hell for her and that she was going to go back to Florida to move in with her Mom. She's single you know, so she had nothing holding her here other than this job. When she became a bit of a pariah with certain people because of McCoy, she decided to get out of town. It's a darned shame really. She was a great worker," Bob said with a sigh. "I am glad for her though. I think she made the right choice."

"My God! There is absolutely no excuse for Doug's behavior. The only good thing is that Hugh Braxton did the right thing and let the pervert go!" Max exclaimed.

"Yes, Max. I agree. And I can tell you that it has certainly given me a new outlook on women in the workplace and how we should treat them," said the new president of Maleo Industries, Bob Martin.

Sexual harassment and diminution of the value of women have been common practices in North American business for centuries. I am happy to say that the frequency of overt displays of gender bias has reduced with each passing year over the past few decades. However it is a fact that the more things change, the more they stay the same...

****

I have already mentioned that I hear very little about the popularity or notoriety of female CEO's. When major corporations are caught in the throes of impropriety or financial difficultly, very few women are mentioned in the resultant news. In fact, few if any of the major news-making corporations have women at the helm, so very few have an opportunity to make a difference or get into trouble. Although women make up almost half of the entire American workforce, in 1996 only one *Fortune 500* company had a CEO or President who was a woman. In 2005 there were eight women running *Fortune 500* companies and in 2007 the number rose to a total of twelve. Although some progress was made during the eleven years mentioned, as of 2007, women were in charge of only 2.4% of all *Fortune 500* companies. Given the fact that women make up almost 50 percent of the workforce, there seems to be a disparity between their work effort and their ability to move into top jobs. In fact, in 2005, 67 Fortune 500 companies had no women at all on their lists of corporate officers. It follows then that the executive committees of those companies presumably made major decisions that affected thousands or even millions of people every day without the benefit of even one female vote, voice, or opinion. Clearly this subject merits more investigation.

Various studies of a significant number of American businesses have indicated that femininity even has a bearing on corporate mergers and acquisitions. On average, female executives tend to value businesses that they wish to acquire, lower than men do. They are more cautious and are less likely to be overwhelmed by the desire for a merger than men. They prefer to choose caution to generosity and haste. In addition to that, corporations that have women on their executive boards or committees are generally purchased for lower prices than those that are completely controlled by men. This tendency is so pronounced that the value of businesses reduces proportionately with the number of women sitting on their boards. The more women on the board—the lower the purchase price of the company. Don't tell me that this is not a man's world! Clearly when men get into a negotiation their hunter-gatherer instincts kick in and they are compelled to exercise their financial muscles in order to show off their superior power. That phenomenon

WAYNE KEHL

could be compared to a silverback male gorilla pounding his chest to prove his supremacy and show his contempt for weaker male gorillas. Women on the other hand, are not afraid to walk away from a deal if it does not meet their standards or expectations. They have no desire to appear superior by spending more money than they feel is appropriate in order to make a deal happen. In stark contrast to their male counterparts, they will not be taken advantage of by their own ego.

Here are some facts that might help explain why the work efforts of women have not brought them to the pinnacle of corporate control. Women tend to dominate jobs that are less likely to bring them to a position where advancement to senior management is likely or even appropriate. For example, in 2006, 96.9 percent of all secretaries and administrative assistants in the United States were women; 91.3 percent of all nurses were ladies; 90.3 percent of all accounting clerks and 94.2 percent of all childcare workers were female. Not surprisingly, 93.4 percent of all hairdressers and 97.7 percent of all preschool and kindergarten teachers were members of the fairer sex. Can you see a pattern here? Clearly, there are a lot of jobs that are stereotypically oriented toward females. As women are gravitating toward those jobs, men are putting up their hands and saying, "No way!" How many testosterone packing, burly, men have you seen as receptionists or nurses? How many do you expect to see in the future? Of course, there are exceptions but they are few and far between. Note that most of the jobs I have mentioned put women into a position of servitude. They are helping children, providing a service for adults, or supporting more successful men. While women are serving others, they are not building a basis for advancement. Conversely, while men are refusing to take on female-dominated positions, they are building a basis for advancement and greater fortune for themselves.

I spent most of my adult life in the general insurance business in Canada. I started out working part time in my Dad's office while going to high school and over the following forty years, worked my way up to vice president of operations for a major international firm. In excess of 70 percent of all people employed in the general insurance business in Canada are women. Most of those women work in support roles. The decision makers and highly paid sales people are mainly men. As a young man I had the opportunity to visit the head and branch offices of many insurance companies. I always marveled at the preponderance of women in those big offices. Head offices in high-rise buildings generally had huge open areas, broken up into partitioned cubicles or open areas with desks placed row upon row. Around the perimeter of those open areas were the windows and of course that is where the enclosed offices were. You guessed it…the open areas in the central part of the offices were populated mostly by women. The offices with doors and floor-to-ceiling window views were populated almost completely by men. I recall one company that thought it was being quite revolutionary and liberal when it put the open areas near the window and the offices in the central core. That way, the women, (who were generally paid less and worked longer hours) had the benefit of window views while the highly paid men were forced to slave away in spacious, comfortable, hardwood paneled offices without any personal window views at all. I do not want to offend any of my old insurance cronies, male or female, but I do find it surprising that very intelligent, otherwise highly evolved executives could not understand the obvious gender biases that were brought to the fore by simple interior design and placement of furniture. It was common practice to put men in offices and women in a *bullpen*. It was assumed that if you hired a man, you had to provide him with a private office. If a woman miraculously made it into an office however, she was put up on pedestal by her male bosses and pointed to as an example of the liberal and progressive attitude of the firm. Successful women often did not become successful because of talent, but rather because of the need of their twentieth century employers to have a *token woman* in an office. That is not to say that they were not talented…only that talent was not the defining factor in their success.

It is safe to say that in North America, women are paid less than men. In fact, on average, women are paid 20 to 30 percent less than men. In some cases women actually doing the same job, putting in the same effort, and producing as much product as men are rewarded with a smaller pay check. A gender wage gap exists that is very real and cannot be denied by even the most jaded of experts. Statistics can be misleading however and it must be acknowledged that women gravitate to jobs that pay less than men. Most truck drivers for example are men while most restaurant servers are women. Since truckers are paid more than waitresses the wage percentile in this example averages downward for women. My largest concern is for situations where equal pay for equal work still does not exist. Many male bosses will pay women less, if and when they can with no regret and no penalty. Some experts also believe that there is so much *overcrowding* of women in traditional female jobs that an overabundance of supply has weakened demand. That disparity quite naturally drives the wages for those jobs downward.

One of the issues that can prevent women from advancing in the workplace is maternity. As much as we love them and as much as we need them to repopulate the planet, babies tend to be unwanted interruptions in the progress of business. Of course, men do not have to worry about becoming pregnant and they seldom leave their jobs to nurture their children. For that reason, women are often passed over as future CEO's, Presidents, managers, or even as regular full time employees. The inevitable career interruption created by maternity is simply not acceptable to many employers. Since mothers and fathers both have responsibility for, and benefit of, their mutual children, it seems somewhat unfair that women must put their jobs on hold, risking uncertain career paths due to maternity. Nevertheless, it is still assumed that when a pregnancy occurs, the mother will be the one to leave her job for an extended period of time or even permanently. There have been attempts made by various Governments in progressive countries to encourage paternity leave for men in order to equalize child-rearing responsibilities but in most cases it is still women who make the sacrifice.

Another reason that women have difficulty generating the same level of income and prestige as their male counterparts appears to be their own lifestyle selection process. Many women prioritize children and family over career. Due to that they will avoid long shifts, travel, and inflexible hours of work when choosing a career or seeking advancement. When the male bosses are faced with the choice of advancing a man who will sacrifice his home life and his family for his career, as opposed to a woman who won't, they will generally choose the man. Businesses have shareholders and boards of directors who demand growth and huge returns on investment. Because of that, no matter how evolved, or liberal a CEO or manager is, he or she will be forced by financial considerations to accept gender inequality…or risk losing his or her own position. Until the world changes its view of exactly what gender equality should look like, we cannot expect men and women to receive the same treatment or be offered the same opportunities.

It is a fact some businesses could not survive financially if equal pay for equal work actually existed. In many cases women will work for less because their intent is to provide a secondary income for their families. In some cases, the male in the relationship generates all of the income required to feed, house, and clothe his family. The woman's income may either be a *top up* to improve lifestyle or just to provide a personal income for the female worker. In many cases in North America today, families cannot live an acceptably normal lifestyle without both spouses working to bring in enough income to pay the bills. Businesses that thrive on light-duty, low paid, shift work such as call centers, fast food restaurants, and janitorial firms would struggle to survive if it became law that both members of every household must be paid the same. Many businesses with a large percentage of women who do computer processing and paperwork for male sales people and executives would have to close their doors if everyone was paid the same. The trend toward lower pay for women is so ingrained in North America that some business owners and company presidents that I have known have blatantly stated, (behind closed doors) that they hire women specifically because they will work for less money than men.

A lot of this may seem like sad commentary on North American business ethics and morals. However, I am pleased to say that many of the male executives I know want to improve things for women. Many want to see the talents of women and men rewarded on the same basis. Many male CEO's wish to see their companies evolve through elimination of all prejudice. Never in my forty years in business have I seen such generalized concern for fairness and equality in the workplace. Stick with us, Ladies…we *are* evolving and with patience you will attain your rightful places in business and industry in no time. What you must NOT do if you want to progress in your career is to pretend that all of the facts that I have provided here are unimportant or invalid and that women are simply the victims of mistreatment by cruel and unjust men. Men have ruled the world for a very long time and rightly or wrongly they still hold the majority of power. If you accept that the workplace is evolving and if you contribute in a positive, supportive fashion you will find that the men you work with will respond in kind. Remember that men in positions of power are generally very dominant and will only respond positively to a challenge if it is well thought out and if a reasonable alternative is offered. I have seen far too many examples of people expecting negative behavior to generate positive results. In fact, a positive result almost never emerges from negativity. If you rudely tell your boss he is unfair…he might treat you unfairly. If you accuse him of being a male chauvinist…he might become one. If you threaten to quit…he might thank you! Utilize the common sense, patience, talent, and charm that you were born with to move your workplace in a positive direction and you will reap the rewards that almost always result from positive energy.

One final thought on equality: When a woman feels that she is the victim of male chauvinism or gender bias, she should first ask herself if the poor treatment she is suffering has anything to do with discrimination or if it has more to do with her own performance. When people of either gender are working in jobs they are fundamentally not suited to, they tend to perform poorly. Occasionally in these cases a manager is forced to perform disciplinary action or even termination. From time to time I have heard poor performing females use their gender as an excuse for the discipline or termination…choosing to ignore that fact that they had been doing a poor job. Poor performance *is* poor performance and no workplace should suffer from it due to the fear of unfounded claims of gender discrimination.

A few women will use gender bias or male chauvinism as the reason for almost any negative situation they come across. I once had a female client call me to complain about the service she received from a male manager in one of the offices that I was responsible for. She stated loudly and clearly that he ignored her until she forced him to talk to her and then he treated her rudely while providing extremely poor service. A large part of her diatribe revolved around her feeling that the manager had no respect for women and was clearly a male chauvinist. Knowing the manager as an extremely kind and compassionate man, I was shocked at what I was hearing. Once I had promised the distraught woman that I would get to the bottom of the situation, I called the manager and asked him for his side of the story. What unfolded was a tale of a woman who had been treated with the utmost of care and compassion and a service level that was above and beyond the norm. Satisfied that my manager had performed his duty as a service provider in his usual exemplary fashion, but wanting to be fair I called the lady back. When I explained the details of our service policy and how my manager had actually gone above and beyond it, she refused to accept my perceptions of the events and indicated that the manager was lying. She then went on to tell me that many men she deals with treat her with disdain and that she often had to complain about them. She further advised that she would not stop complaining about men until she had made a difference in the world and until women took their rightful place in society. Sensing that this lady had no intention of accepting my view of the situation, I offered to refund a portion of her insurance premium as a courtesy and asked her to return to our office to speak with the manager about the service he provided to her and to receive her refund. She refused. She demanded that I have a woman look after her, because she had no intention of ever speaking to *that man* again.

I mention this situation here because in my mind it was clear that the lady's complaints were intended to attack a man who was doing everything he could to satisfy her needs rather than to overcome any alleged service issues. I have mentioned it also to illustrate the fact that there are some women in the world who have lost touch with reality where male chauvinism is concerned and who do more harm than good to the women's movement. Interestingly, if this woman had called me to compliment my manager on a job well done, she might have advanced the cause of women dramatically. My manager would have considered her a great person who was so generous that she would take time out of her day to perform an act of kindness. Instead, because of her overt negativity, she left a bad taste in the mouth of my kindly manager about the advancement of women's liberation. Not only would he prefer never to be forced to deal with that particular woman ever again, but he became a tad gun-shy about dealing with women in general. Her actions had the opposite effect of what she intended because she acted unreasonably and without integrity. People of either gender cannot advance their cause through outrageous claims and negative intentions. As a footnote to this story, I spoke with some of the women who work in that office and they advised me that they sympathized with their manager because the woman in question was quite cruel to him. They also confirmed my suspicions that he had acted professionally and compassionately throughout the woman's unreasonable attack upon him.

The bottom line, Ladies, is that men in the workplace are sensitive to the terms, *male chauvinism, gender bias, and women's liberation*. Because of that, it is advisable for women who wish to advance in the workforce to be absolutely certain that some form of gender discrimination *does* actually exist before they make statements that might harm the men they wish to reform. If you find one of your female coworkers making such claims unfairly, you will do the cause of women a great service if you ask them to stop. On the other hand, if gender discrimination really does exist, you owe it to yourself and your fellow-women to take it to the highest authority necessary to have it eliminated.

Men seem not to be as sensitive to gender discrimination as women are, but the good men among us want to put an end to it. Male chauvinists are a crafty bunch, and they often get away with negative treatment of women for years with total impunity. Most of us guys don't want chauvinism to exist at all. We want the word, *chauvinism* to disappear from the English language. It is embarrassing, and we know that it is simply wrong. Hence, if you are aware of chauvinism at work, take the evidence to someone you trust and don't stop forcing the issue until the bad treatment has been eradicated. If you can't make it stop, and you can't find anyone to deal with the problem in a positive way, you should leave that place of employment and find one that practices equality. There are more and more fully evolved workplaces springing up every day so don't allow yourself to become a victim by settling for poor treatment.

In the first chapter of this book I talked about a number of women who were quite famous and successful in a variety of ways. Those women did not *settle* and they did not allow male chauvinism to hold them back. They acted with impeccable integrity at all times and they forged on when life was at its bleakest. Women, who want to be successful by male standards, should follow the lead of those famous women. When they do that, they will take the world by storm. With respect Ladies, please do not allow the men in your life to be the reason or the excuse for your own lack of success.

I cannot end this chapter on women at work without talking about sexual harassment. Although each jurisdiction has its own interpretation, the word "harassment" when used in the workplace is generally defined as *unwelcome comments or conduct based on sex, race or other legally protected characteristics that unreasonably interferes with an employee's work performance or is intimidating, hostile or offensive to another person.* Examples of sexual harassment include but are not limited to, *leering or staring in a sexually suggestive manner; offensive remarks about appearance, clothing or body parts; unwanted touching, pinching, patting, or intentional brushing against another person's body; telling sexual or lewd jokes; making sexual gestures, making unwanted sexual advances, displaying or circulating sexually suggestive emails, letters, notes, images or other materials.* Note that the harassment need not necessarily be directed at the person who ultimately makes the complaint. Any of these scenarios that may be overheard or viewed from a distance that make another person uncomfortable can be construed as harassment. Note too, that sexual harassment is not the sole domain of men. Women can in fact be guilty of harassing men or other women should they be guilty of initiating any of the scenarios noted above.

The distaff side of society has men *running scared* on the sexual harassment front. There has been so much media attention focused on it that men are often afraid to be too friendly or simply act like themselves around women at work. As much as harassment should not be tolerated, like chauvinism, it must be real and tangible before it is acted upon. As we evolve, we are beginning to find that some women tend to mimic men in the workplace in order to move up the corporate ladder. That evolutionary behavior seems to include more cursing, more talking about sex, more leering at men, more sexually suggestive remarks about men, (and *to* men) on an ever-increasing level. While men are trying to be more politically correct and cautious about how they speak to women, many ladies are reversing the roles by becoming more provocative and by adopting the chauvinistic ways of men. Women must be cautious when acting like *good old boys* during conversations with men since their more liberal attitudes might be misconstrued as promiscuity or even sexual harassment against men. A more liberal and less *ladylike* presentation at work might backfire into an unexpected, negative scenario. It might also lead to overt sexual harassment. At this point I think it is prudent for me to remind my readers that I am not making personal judgments with these comments. My intent is only to point out the reality of male/female relationships in the twenty first century.

It is important to understand that anti-discrimination laws are not inflexible, universal codes of civility. In other words the laws do not prohibit simple teasing, offhand comments, or isolated incidents that are not intended to be serious. The conduct must be so offensive as to alter the working conditions of the person being harassed. The harassment must actually create a tangible and negative effect on the life of the complainant or be sufficient to create a hostile work environment. In other words, people who have a bad sense of humor or a bad attitude are not to be considered guilty of sexual harassment unless it becomes an extremely serious or harmful matter for another employee. Before anyone brings a formal charge of sexual harassment, they should document their complaints and make certain they can formally back up the justifications for it. A charge of sexual harassment can end a career or destroy a life so it must be taken very seriously.

The final words on harassment and the final words on women at work are this: Always remain calm and think before reacting. Always respond to improper behavior rationally and without anger. Bring complaints of discrimination or harassment against men only when you know it is real and deliberate but never allow genuine discrimination or harassment to go unnoticed. Always take the high road. When faced with adversity or prejudice, forge on with dignity. Men and women *can* get along at work if they try a little harder and women *can* move up corporate ladders if they practice patience while pushing aside stereotypes and refusing to accept anything less than what they deserve. Persistence and consistently good performance will win over gender bias or negativity fostered by old stereotypes and chauvinistic attitudes every time. Just think about Elizabeth Fry or Mother Teresa. They acted with gentility and kindness in a male dominated world at times and in places where women were more likely to fail than succeed...yet succeed they did!

Clothes don't make the man...
But they might make the woman!

CHAPTER 4
Women and Clothing

As Bob Martin walked down the third floor hallway of the Maleo Industries head office his head was held high and his gait carried a newfound swagger. He was thrilled that the board of directors had selected him as the new president after Doug McCoy was let go. Unbeknownst to him, the board, led by Hugh Braxton chose Bob because he was the least likely to create problems. Bob Martin was known to be kind, fair, and soft-spoken. He had no obvious prejudices and he almost never said anything bad about another human being. In short, he was politically correct. The board had no confusion that Bob could ever be a superstar like his predecessor, but after the news of Doug McCoy had gotten around to various clients and suppliers, they knew they needed to send a message to the business world that they had seen the error of their ways and were willing to appoint a less offensive leader to top job.

Bob grew up in a great environment where he and his siblings were treated with respect and kindness by his parents at all times. He was taught to have respect and empathy for everyone that came into his life. As a child, his youthful enthusiasm and naïveté occasionally got him into trouble because he was easily led by neighborhood kids whose family values were not as positive as his. Whenever he was caught in a prank or in the act of saying something inappropriate, his parents would take him aside and lecture him on the value of kindness and good morals. The devil didn't stand *a chance of taking over the soul of Bob Martin. In fact, his upbringing made him almost too nice for business but despite his ductile pliancy, his quiet, raw determination carried him all the way to the President's chair at Maleo. The board trusted him and hoped dearly that he would be tough enough to do the job.*

Generally, the ladies in the office liked Bob a lot. He was an attractive man who did not flaunt his status. Some women simply enjoyed his kind charm while others were attracted to him because of his newfound power at Maleo Industries. He was too naïve to notice when he was being flirted with but he was man enough to notice the appealing feminine attributes of some of the women who came on to him. He liked the women he worked with but he would never think of becoming involved with any of them romantically. He was happily married and simplistically believed that the good-looking ladies who consistently hung around him were only being nice. One of the more attractive women in the office, an accounting clerk by the name of Joy Stonely, was not only pressing and persistent in her flirtatious stalking of Bob; she was also incredibly audacious in her manner of dress. She consistently dressed in revealing tops, short skirts, visible undergarments and lace stockings. When in the presence of Bob, she often leaned forward deliberately and overtly in order to expose even more cleavage than usual and she always managed to adopt a provocative pose whether sitting or standing. Despite the fact that Bob often got an eyeful of Joy's physical charms, he seemed oblivious to the fact that she was making every possible attempt to arouse him.

One day as Joy and Bob were reviewing the monthly production numbers in Bob's office Alex Smithson walked in unannounced and interrupted them. Not only was Alex a tough businessman, he was honest, pragmatic and always called a spade a spade. Unlike Bob Martin, he could NOT be described as naïve. As he approached the door he was both shocked and titillated to see Bob seated in his high back recliner with Joy standing beside him, leaning over, her face only inches from Bob's as she pointed to a line on a report. Alex hardly noticed either of their faces, as he stared at Joy's almost completely exposed breasts hanging pendulously over the desk, swaying slightly as she moved her finger back and forth across the report. Her blouse was partially unbuttoned and her bra was so brief that he imagined all it would take was a little sneeze for both breasts to bounce completely out of her clothing and onto the desk. Snapping himself out of that fantasy, Alex who had not been noticed by Bob or Joy as he stood silently in the office doorway, cleared his throat to get their attention.

The sound, 'ah hem' came out of Alex as he held his fist to his mouth to make his throat-clearing ruse complete. Alex and Joy looked up simultaneously and in almost perfect unison said, "Hi Alex!" Joy, blushing, stood up straight and faced Alex. She looked down at herself, and realizing that she was probably showing more cleavage than might be considered acceptable in the office, fastened one additional button on her blouse. Bob continued sitting, oblivious to Joy's embarrassment and Alex's obvious intrigue.

"Hey, what's up Alex?" Bob said with a smile in his voice.

"Oh nothing, Bob! It can wait if you two are busy," Alex said mischievously.

"I was just leaving. You can have your meeting now," Joy said hurriedly as she strutted toward the door in her spiky-heeled, red patent leather shoes.

When Joy had closed the door behind her, Alex turned to Bob with a big grin on his face. He walked over to Bob's desk still smiling and when he was within a foot of the desk he leaned over and whispered, "Holy crap, Bob! Are you doing her?"

Bob was shocked, but as naïve as ever, he assumed that Alex was joking. "What are you talking about Alex? You're such a kidder!" he laughed.

Seeing that he had to shock Bob with the facts of life, Alex spoke loudly, "Who's kidding who, Bob? Joy's boobs were falling out of her blouse and she was rubbing herself all over you like a new puppy. I would have thought that after what happened to Doug McCoy you would be a little more careful about messing around with the staff!"

Immediately defensive and angry, Bob could feel the blood rushing to his face as his pulse began to quicken. "That's crazy, Alex! Why are you trying to cause trouble for me? I thought we were friends!" he retorted with obvious pain in his voice.

"Oh for God's sake, Bob that woman has been coming on to you ever since you got the President's job and everyone knows it!" Alex yelled. Bob slumped back in his chair, obviously hurt and completely disarmed. It was clear to him that he should listen to what Alex had to say. "I am speaking as a friend now, Bob. She dresses like a prostitute and shows off more skin than is legal in most states every time she has a meeting with you. Every woman in the place is talking about it and the guys are taking bets on how long it will be before Hugh Braxton comes in here and cans you too. Jeez, you're so naïve, Bob. I can't believe that you haven't noticed and I can't believe that you are risking your career like this!"

As Bob looked up at Alex his eyes were glassy and his face had gone very pale. "Oh my God, Alex…I never even thought about it, but you might be right. If my wife ever got wind of this she would be devastated. What should I do? I can't even think straight right now. Help me out here," he pleaded.

Alex walked over to the window and surveyed the view for a moment before turning back to Bob, saying calmly, "Get rid of her, Bob. Just get rid of her."

Sexual chemistry and sexual attraction are common in the workplace. Even though both of these elements of human nature are evident whenever human beings get together, the union of the two can create a hazardous phenomenon for men and women alike. Many careers have been destroyed by overt sexuality and much caution is in order. Let's explore how women can avoid some of Joy Stonely's mistakes.

****

Now, this is where I will probably wander into dangerous territory. As I peruse the photographs of successful businesswomen in various publications, I find them mostly attractive, physically fit, well dressed, and well groomed. I am pleased to say that I find the same is generally true for photos of successful businessmen. However, as a person who has known thousands of male bosses and hundreds of male CEO's and presidents of corporations, I must say that female beauty is often a factor in female success. It seems as though men prefer to advance women to senior roles only if they present an image that is acceptable to other men. This discussion brings us back to hormones and male/female attraction. Men like to be seen with attractive women by their sides. A man with an attractive woman at his *beck and call* is considered successful by world standards. There is a much-used expression that says, *"Behind every successful man stands a woman."* Although it is meant to be a positive statement, this expression bears testimony to the fact that the world assumes that women will always be subservient to, and supportive of men...*as long as they remain behind them*! In the business world, as in private, men want to be in the company of sexually attractive women. Women who do not attempt to present themselves as attractive, well groomed, and professional in appearance and who are not in favor with their male superiors because of it, have little chance of advancing in our male dominated business world. That trend is changing to some extent as a few determined, aggressive women are forsaking North American gender discrimination standards while remaining true to themselves. However, as is witnessed by the fact that very few females make it to the top of the *Fortune 500* list, progress is very slow.

Have you ever thought about *why* women's clothing is designed the way it is? I am certainly not a *fashionista*, but I have paid a lot of attention to the design and form of clothing throughout my life. Ever changing fashion trends generally maintain one common element...*sex*. Think about my earlier discussion of hormones and reproduction. The clothing of women and men is clearly designed to emphasize their sexuality. Men's suits have broad shoulders and even, shoulder pads to create an appearance of strength and male dominance. Those North American icons, *blue denim jeans* are cut with a tight posterior area in order to emphasize the sexuality of that part of men and women. Almost all pants are cut right up and into the crotch area so that there is little doubt about what lies beneath. From a practical perspective, it is really quite inconvenient to have clothing that fits very tightly in the crotch area but throughout modern times, tight crotches have persisted through various and sundry style eras. For men, clothing emphasizes their ability to produce sperm and protect their woman while providing food and shelter. For women, clothing is like a picture frame that contains a beautiful painting of reproductive prowess.

The word *fit*, when applied to clothing, suggests sexuality all by itself. Clothing generally fits well when it is tight and clinging to the body it envelops. Often it seems so tight that it might cut off all blood circulation while other times it drapes in such a way that it emphasizes the size and shape of a particular body part. I recently went on a weight loss program in order to maintain better health in my senior years. Although I was successful in losing weight, what I had not considered during the process was that my clothing might not fit as well as it did when I was heavier. The most common comment I received from people I know was that they could tell I had lost weight because my pants were baggy around my butt. I must admit that I was a tad shocked by that...partly because I was unaware of it myself and partly because I heard it from several individuals. I had to wonder why those people were looking at my butt at all and I began to fear that random people were peering at my butt and analyzing its size and shape on a regular basis. Suddenly, my butt became an integral element of my personal insecurity system. I became filled with previously non-existent worry and wonder if my butt was somewhat attractive or actually quite disgusting. I should point out that it was mainly women who made those shocking comments. I attribute that to the fact that most men would not want to be caught looking at or commenting on another man's butt. In fact, due to the competitive nature of men, I suspect that any man, who noticed that my pants had a baggy butt, would feel much better about himself knowing that his pants fit his butt much better than mine did. The last thing he would want to do is tell me about it since at that moment in time he was beating me in at least one thing…the unspoken, yet ever present, *great-butt* contest.

Recently I was speaking about dieting and weight loss with a female co-worker. She was interested in what process I utilized in order to lose weight and what sort of exercise regime I was following. I talked a lot about sugar, carbohydrates, treadmills, rowing machines and I briefly touched on the inches I had removed from my waistline. As I was speaking, I noticed her face had taken on a look of concern that verged on worry. I assumed that I was boring her or that I had touched a chord in her that brought about some unpleasant thoughts. Before I could ask what was bothering her, she blurted out, "I'm just not sure if I want to lose that much weight." Because I had become a bit of an evangelist for healthy living, I began to discuss the health and longevity benefits of a good weight loss and exercise plan. She listened politely and then said, "I know all that but I don't want to lose weight off my butt! I like my butt and I want it to stay the way it is!" When I finished laughing I pointed out to her that I suspected her butt would reduce in size and proportion to the rest of her body and although smaller, it would be suitable for her frame. She gave me a look of disdain, shook her head, and wandered out of my office muttering about her butt. The significance of that story for me is that the hips and butt of a woman are really just physiological indications of childbearing ability...yet in modern times, hips and butts have become so integral to a woman's persona that some women look at their butts as an important element of their physical beauty and sexuality. Many women have huge self-confidence issues surrounding various body parts...the gluteus maximus being one of them. As a typical naive man, I had never considered the fact that women might inspect and analyze their own butts to any great extent. Of course, further research with the women in my life cleared that naïveté up for me in no uncertain terms. Female sexuality in the twenty first century has evolved well beyond the simple reproductive process. Women are extremely aware of the power of it and that awareness creates the behavior that fuels the fashion industry and drives testosterone wild.

The folks who create fashion have two very powerful elements to play to...sex and competition. Often women will dress to emphasize their sexuality in an effort to impress the men around them, but just as often they will dress to impress other women with their fashion sense or their wealth and status. Most men know little about fashion, so the fact that a famous, popular designer created a particular article of clothing is lost on them. All they really care about is how the woman looks in her clothing. When a man looks at a woman he sees someone who is sexy, well dressed, professionally dressed, poorly dressed, shabbily dressed or dressed like a man. No matter which element he perceives, he is seldom wondering if the garment or one like it might be displayed in a Rodeo Drive shop window. He feels no curiosity or concern about the status of the clothing. All he feels is an attraction or revulsion based on the cut and relative sexiness of the outfit. Because of that, a woman may be wearing an incredibly expensive outfit designed by a famous designer but because it lacks the sex appeal and body enhancing qualities that a man wants, he will find it forgettable or simply *ugly*.

Women on the other hand, can impress other women and garner a huge amount of respect and respectability by wearing clothing that is both costly and stylish. Appearance in terms of clothing is a matter of major personal competition amongst western women…one always wanting to dress better than, or at least as well as the other. Many women know one designer from the other and are impressed by clothing that is on the cutting edge of fashion trends, just as men know and are impressed by the design and options of a Chevrolet Corvette or a cordless drill. Women who can afford to dress in expensive designer clothing will drop the name of the designer of a particular item that they may be wearing in an effort to prove their good taste and status. When they mention a particular designer to another woman, that woman will be impressed. She might hate the other woman for her vanity but she will be impressed nonetheless. When she drops a designer's name to a man, chances are he will shrug his shoulders and say, "So what?" Women who cannot afford designer clothing will still compete with other women for the title of *best dressed* by wearing copies, knock-offs, or clothing that mimics current fashion trends. Again, when they wish to be stylish, they are generally dressing to impress other women rather than men. Unfortunately, if they are dressing for men, unless the outfit is cut to show some skin they will be tragically disappointed.

It is a bonus for women when they are able to find clothing that is both sexy and stylish, but often that can have negative repercussions as well. One might well think that other women would appreciate a manner of dress that is attractive to men while meeting current fashion trends. However, where fashion is concerned women tend to be every bit as competitive as men, and a woman who tends to dress in clothing that is overtly sexy, may be criticized or shunned despite any designer labels. Often the source of the criticism has more to do with envy or ego than it does with disapproval of the style or righteous indignation based in religion or morals. I have often heard some very nice women being called tramps or sluts by other women simply because of their manner of dress. Society has created some confusing rules and some folks tend to randomly grab one or another of the various cultural regulations off the shelf in order to compete with other people and win through critical observation and outright rudeness.

Trends in female clothing options are seemingly endless. A quick glance around any neighborhood in any city will reveal everything from classic business garb; to sporty spandex; to grungy, ripped jeans and tee shirts; to exotic oriental or middle-eastern styles; to military uniforms; to cowboy or farmer styles; to fashionable and sophisticated evening wear. You can find most of these styles in almost every North American office any day of the week. As a manager for many years I had the job of interpreting the dress code for my various offices and casting judgment over the suitability of the clothing of my staff. In the seventies and eighties when skirts went from mini to micro, I gave up that job to whichever female in my office had the highest rank at any given time. It occurred to me that since I knew nothing about fashion and therefore nothing about what might be acceptable, my aging male perceptions might not be current or fair to my female employees. I was often embarrassed to the point of looking away, red-faced when speaking with young ladies as they faced me, seated, legs apart wearing micro mini-skirts. The sights I became privy to in those situations put me into a position of compromise with myself. I wondered if I should say something; if I should look away; or if I should just leave the scene of the crime. In order to avoid prolonged embarrassment I generally tended to make those visits very short indeed. Now, when I witness female clothing that seems inappropriate to the work environment, I will ask another woman if she too feels that it is inappropriate. If she answers in the affirmative, I will ask her to deal with it. If she answers in the negative, I will apologize for my ignorance of current fashion trends and wander back to my office. You see, Ladies you have men at a disadvantage because our primeval, testosterone-driven instincts make us want to respond naturally to the stimulus you place before us, but political correctness and workplace etiquette make us weak and confused.

Lets talk about breasts. Female human breasts are almost perfectly designed for the production and delivery of life-giving milk to human offspring. One must assume that the larger the breasts are, the more milk they might produce. Taken one step further, when men are observing and being titillated by female breasts they are being driven by a primeval desire to mate with a female who can produce and nurture a family of strong, healthy children. That reproductive need has forever been translated as sexual desire. It has also created opportunities for the preponderance of breast enhancing clothing and apparatus that exists in North America today. Brassieres of various varieties have been invented to push up, push together, hold up, and enlarge the breasts of the wearer. There are padded bras, breast pads, (commonly known to men as *falsies*) and stick on breast enlargements that may be worn with an already-enhancing undergarment. I am sure that some designer or undergarment professional, somewhere in the world is designing the next great bra as I write this. The bottom line here is that the fashion industry has made billions of dollars emphasizing female milk production organs. In addition to external enhancement apparatus, North American women are having potentially dangerous breast enhancement surgeries in ever increasing numbers every day. I hate to be a *party pooper,* Ladies but you don't need surgery to attract a good man. Men are attracted to women of all shapes and sizes and there is no particular body part that will make him ask for your hand in marriage or even make him ask you out on a second date. You might attract a man on a superficial level by displaying your body in an attractive way, but ultimately all you will accomplish is the activation of his primitive male instincts. If you want to have a relationship with a man, you must communicate with him in a way that appeals to him. Communication between two people is much more stimulating and enduring than any sexual encounter. People who get together primarily because of a good sex life, will generally not last as a couple and they will probably not mate for life. That phenomenon is a contributing factor in today's alarmingly high North America's divorce rate.

The dimensions of breasts, hips, butts, waistlines and legs have become the source of personal insecurity and stress for many North American women. Modern media and society have created standards that are almost impossible to attain but women will continue to try to achieve perfection long after I have passed from this earthly existence. I won't change the world with this book, but I do want all women to understand that ordinary, average, good men do not buy into the fashion industry's take on beauty. It is a fact that we respect women for all of the *right* reasons, despite any apparent dimensional or physiological challenges.

Moving away from the sexual elements of clothing, I want to touch on professionalism as it relates to dress. Earlier in this chapter I mentioned some of the specific types of dress that women might be wearing at any moment in time. It is a fact that men and women in an advanced age bracket that spans from approximately 40 to 60 years of age, control most North American businesses. In other words older folks, *Boomers* and *Generation X* people, are calling the shots for employees at all levels. We have already learned that there are more men than women in control of business and finance so it is important that we understand what men think about the way women dress at work. It is a fact that the more professionally a person dresses, the more likely they are to progress. That applies to men and women equally. Nowhere is that more true than in the so-called, *white collar* businesses. Welders wear overalls, sports teams and military staff, wear uniforms, and nurses wear scrubs. Many occupations require a specific and obvious manner of dress but office workers are not so lucky. The smartest accountant might fail to make it to the executive level of his or her firm because of a slovenly appearance and a superior performer may be snubbed for a promotion due to wrinkled, poorly fitting clothing. Unfortunately, many people seem not to be at all aware of what their appearance should be. I have watched society's clothing standards evolve over the past 5 decades and what I have observed is confusion and a lack of direction. In the nineteen fifties and nineteen sixties, men in offices wore white dress shirts with ties and business suits. There were no other options. That was the uniform of success. As time passed, suits gave way to sport jackets and slacks while white shirts gave way to shirts of many colors. Ties are all but disappearing from North American business. In the nineteen nineties, businesses all over North America came up with the idea of *casual Friday*, which allowed acceptance of blue denim jeans in the office environment one day of every week. What I am seeing now is a complete erosion of business clothing styles with men wearing everything from open collared shirts with dress slacks to jeans and tee shirts in the office. Women have had just as difficult a road to follow. In the forties and fifties, women most often wore below-the-knee-length dresses or business suits consisting of a jacket, skirt and a blouse with a suitably high neck line. Interestingly, in those days women were not generally permitted to wear pants or slacks of any kind to work. I believe that men felt that women should look like women at work and therefore they could not wear pants since those were considered the exclusive garb of men...just another hint of male subjugation of women from the past. As time passed, standards changed. As the fashion industry grew and the media focused more on women's clothing it was inevitable that women's clothing options would evolve...and evolve they have!

In the new millennium it is important that female employees who wish to advance to dizzying heights in corporations dress in clothing that enhances the fact that they are female but is not so provocative that it can be considered *sexy*. Business suits of matching jackets and skirts or matching jackets and pants are always favorable but not necessary for success. No matter what they wear, women should dress like women; but they must dress like women who came to the office to do a professional job. It is a fact that the fashion industry has driven plunging necklines and décolletage (cleavage) into the workplace over the past few years. Again, I am at a loss as to how to deal with this phenomenon but I find that in almost every office or store I enter during this new millennium, I am faced with female cleavage. That is a matter of style and I imagine there is some socially acceptable amount of cleavage that may be shown, but it is not necessarily the best way for a woman to get into the CEO's chair. As delightful as it is, cleavage makes men uncomfortable in a variety of ways. Many male bosses will opt to communicate with, or even advance a woman who does not compromise his sense of political correctness before one he finds titillating, despite relative performance levels. Communication leads to understanding and understanding can lead to respect. Ultimately, respect in the workplace can lead to advancement. If you are not communicating with your boss because he is afraid that his intentions might appear to be questionable, you are not making the connection you need to make in order to advance your career. Hence, an eye for professional apparel is a great advantage for up-and-coming young businesswomen. Do not make the mistake of making the man who holds the future of your career in his hands uncomfortable by being overtly sexy or unprofessional in your appearance.

Women who wear sweat pants, jogging pants, summer shorts, Capri pants, tee shirts, sweat shirts, or men's clothing to work in an office are almost guaranteed a spot in the *non-advancement* line. Military clothing is great if you are in the Marines but it does not belong on Wall Street any more than Mexican ponchos and cowboy boots do. When I discuss casual clothing in an office environment with some women, they will tell me that they want to be comfortable or even that they have the *right* to be comfortable. What confuses me is why professional clothing is not considered comfortable. I have worn a jacket and tie to work for decades and frankly, I am as comfortable in those clothes as I am in jeans and a tee shirt. I suspect that those people who wish to be comfortable, are really choosing to dress in a fashion that makes them feel more emotionally comfortable rather than comfortable in a physiological way. Overweight people for example, often wear diaphanous, oversized clothing in an attempt to hide their weight problems. That is fine as long as the clothing is suitable to an office environment rather than something that looks like a pup tent or a bed sheet. There are entire store chains dedicated to overweight clothing so wearing something that is inappropriate is not excusable. Some insecure people like to wear bland, unassuming clothing in an attempt to draw attention away from themselves, so as not to be noticed. Again, that is fine as long as the clothing is not something that would be more suitable on a mountain climber or a longshoreman. Some people feel comfortable in sportswear. Great! Go and join a football team but don't wear a team jersey to the office. Others will wear obvious outdoor wear such as plaid hunting shirts and heavy canvas work pants into the office. You have to think that those folks probably have a gun rack and couple of rifles in the back window of their pickup truck, (my apologies to all of the hunters of the world). My point is that the way you dress at home is not necessarily the way you should dress in the office.

The bottom line is that North American women have an endless array of clothing choices. Those who wish to advance in business should give a good deal of consideration to what their employers expect of them. Despite women's rights or the rights of free people everywhere, corporations are run by highly opinionated men and women, who wield an incredible amount of power. They call the shots and they get to choose who will become successful in their firms. They generally want to surround themselves with well-dressed, well-groomed people and they have the right to make that choice. All of the good intentions, hard work, talent and ability that you bring to your job can be totally neutralized or overruled by a sloppy appearance or a fashion faux pas. That might not be acceptable to your value system but it happens in corporations all over the world every day.

Make your life a little easier…give a **lot** of thought to the way you dress…

What do you mean, women can't
join men's clubs?

CHAPTER 5
Women Want It All

When Max McMaster's 'Big Bertha' driver made contact with his pristine, white 'Titleist' ball and he heard the satisfying crack of the cleanly hit golf shot, his face exploded into a beaming smile. "Man, oh man, I love this game!" he exclaimed to his golf partner, Ron Johnson. Ron was Max's next-door neighbor and the two friends had golfed together almost every Wednesday afternoon on Men's day for the previous eleven years.

"That was an amazing shot, Max. I am guessing about three hundred yards; right down the middle, and an easy chip shot onto the green. Man, I wish I could hit like that!" Ron lamented, having driven his ball only about fifty yards into the rough on his earlier tee shot. "I have been playing this damned game for twenty years and I still hit like a girl! Maybe I should put on a skirt and play on Ladies day!"

"Now, now, Ron! You don't hit like a girl or a lady!" Max said with a smirk. "My Mom could outdrive you any day of the week! Ha Ha Ha!"

"Yah, well, your Mom and all of her friends aren't allowed to play here on Men's day! And thank God for that. Frankly I would hate to have women playing here on the one day we get the course to ourselves!" Ron grumbled.

"Not me Ronny. I wouldn't mind seeing some women out here today. What's your problem with women on the golf course?" Max asked as he chipped his ball within a foot of the flag.

"Oh I don't know, Max. It just seems like every time we men want to have something to ourselves, women want to horn in and take it over. Why can't we just do some man things and be left alone by women for a while?" Ron asked

"I hear a lot of that kind of stuff around my office, Ronny. Our former president, Doug McCoy was the worst. I think he actually hated women…even though he tried to sleep with half of our female staff. When he saw a woman on the golf course he would whine and grumble and even go so far as to yell obscenities at them when they were advancing too slowly. Funny thing was, when groups of men moved too slowly, he was fine with it. He was a typical male chauvinist…the kind that gives us all a bad name, Ron and I never enjoyed golfing with him," Max said curtly as he putted out.

Sensing his friend Max was annoyed with him Ron wanted to make amends. "Hey Max, I didn't mean any disrespect to your Mom. She is a great lady and her friends are a blast!" he yelled across the green as he stroked his ball into the hole from four feet out. "Jeez I shot a six on this hole! All of this woman-talk is putting me off my game, Max! I don't have a problem with women in general, I just kind of think that they seem to want to have all of their private female clubs but they won't let us have anything of our own. That's all I'm trying to say."

The two men walked to the next tee box and seeing a foursome still halfway up the next fairway they sat on the bench by the tee box to continue their conversation.

"Ron, I happen to know that you love your wife and you go golfing with her on weekends every chance you get. I also know that you bought her a brand new set of clubs for Christmas three years ago, so golf clearly isn't the problem. Why don't you think of me as your kindly psychologist for a

moment and tell me what your problem is with women?" Max said with
a chuckle before sitting back, waiting for a response.

"You nailed it, Doctor Max. I just don't like the fact that women want
to have everything that men have and they want to have all of their own
exclusive stuff too. It just doesn't seem fair," Ron said as his voice trailed
off.

"I understand your point Ron, but did you ever think that maybe; just
maybe, women aren't getting everything they want from men; that they aren't
breaking through at every level, and that perhaps they are just grabbing onto
anything they can so that they can begin to feel just a little bit equal to men?"
Max asked patiently.

"Oh, I suppose you're right, Doctor Max! Now just get up there and
embarrass me with another one of your big-ass drives!" Ron said with a
smile. As he watched his friend teeing off, Ron thought about their
conversation and silently came to the conclusion that Max was wrong and
he was right…women ARE unfair to men. He was not willing to change
his mind on the subject but he chose not to argue it with his friend, Max any
longer. Their friendship was more important than boring, old, women's
rights. He felt that it was better to save his venom for other men who would
appreciate it more.

Women have been fighting for equality for centuries. Men like
Max McMaster are few and far between and the fight continues
to this very day. Let's take a look at some of the more blatant
examples of gender bias in some of the most surprising places.

****

A big bone of contention between men and women is and
always has been, exclusivity. In previous generations, men had it
all. They could spend time with their wives when it was
convenient to do so but they also enjoyed the luxury of belonging
to exclusive men's clubs, health clubs, and service clubs. In those

days, men ruled their clubs with ironclad superiority. They could have manly conversations about manly things without fear of scrutiny, interruption, or contradiction by women. They could play poker, drink whisky, and talk dirty anytime they wanted to. They could talk about their wives in unflattering or flattering terms with the only people who could understand them completely...*other men.* They could regale their man friends with stories about sporting events, sexual encounters, and gas mileage with complete impunity. They could tell filthy jokes and compare the sizes of various body parts of any number of people in relative comfort. Generally, the only outcome of all that manly behavior was laughter and joyous celebration. They were like primitive cavemen gathering together to compare their kills and make sacrifices to their *man-Gods.* The best thing about men's clubs was that the guys were free to be men in a man's world. Their exclusive clubs were their islands of freedom and their shelters from feminine things. Men loved their exclusive clubs.

Women's liberation changed all of that. Along with voting rights, higher pay, and job equality women began pushing for something that men held sacred. They decided that there should be no exclusive men's clubs. They believed that if the world was truly going to be fair to women, it had to allow them to join men's clubs. The men who belonged to those men's clubs were shocked. How in the name of all that is holy, could women think that they had a right to belong to a club that was founded and chartered as a place for men only? In fact, they wondered *why* women would want to join an exclusive man's club. What possible interest could they have in talking about carburetors and the *Super Bowl?* Did women not know there was nothing going on in men's clubs that women could possibly enjoy? Did they not know that they would be bored to extinction by the conversations and activities that men carried on behind their testosterone-soaked mahogany doors? What were the gals thinking? It just didn't make any sense at all!

As a student of behavior I was compelled to find out just why it was that women felt men's clubs should no longer be men's clubs. The easiest way to find out was to ask the women who wanted to join. In the late nineteen eighties and early nineteen nineties I did exactly that. Whenever I ran into a woman who wanted to join a men's club or was offended by the existence of men's clubs I asked them just exactly why they had such an unrelenting desire to tear down those most powerful and important bastions of western manhood. My research was somewhat inconclusive, since the reasons were many and varied. However, the common thread amongst those I interviewed was, *"It just isn't fair!"* But why was it not fair, I wondered?

One businesswoman I knew was refused membership in a well-known club in a major British Columbia city. That club occupied a classic, traditional turn of the century, stone building. Inside, its walls were clad in dark mahogany paneling and it sported massive hardwood entry doors. Everything in the design of the building was done on a grand, and very manly scale. The furniture was so large and heavy that it was hard for one man to move even a chair around and of course most of it was clad in the finest of leathers. There were poker rooms, cigar rooms, drinking rooms, reading rooms, billiard rooms, and other rooms that could be used for a variety of wholesome, manly activities. It was the classiest place in town and it was a must for every man of importance including high-ranking politicians and the richest of businessmen to belong to it. If you were *somebody* in the community, you had a membership in that club.

The club was for members only, so even men could not pass through its doors without being in the presence of a member. I had a male friend who was a member so I was fortunate enough to enjoy many an afternoon imbibing and speaking of manly things behind those massive doors. I must say I felt very lucky to be able to spend time in a place where various politicians, authors, millionaires, and celebrities of all sorts had spent time before me. My friend the businesswoman was not so lucky. Women were not allowed into most areas of the club even if accompanied by a male member. They were allowed into the dining room with a member, but security was so tight that if they arrived at the club alone, with the intention of meeting a man in the dining room, they had to wait in the lobby until one of the tuxedoed men of service scouted out the subject male member and brought him to the lobby to meet her. This was so that he may *escort* his female companion into the gourmet eatery that men enjoyed without encumbrance every day. It was as if the men were afraid that if the female guests were not escorted, they might run amuck or catch men doing something horrible like discussing politics or playing poker. That bit of indignity was more than most women could bear.

One day while she was expounding on the prejudice and lack of fairness that was being displayed by this age-old British Columbia icon, I asked my female friend why she would want to join a club that apparently discriminated against women so overtly and seemed to display extreme disdain for all members of the fairer sex. My point being that I would expect such an awful place to be boycotted; criticized and avoided by women for its socially unacceptable behavior. I was having trouble understanding what fascination it held for women and why indeed, they would want to have any part of it. Being a man, I also assumed that warm scotch; stinky cigars; and raucous discussions about cubic inch displacement would hold absolutely no interest for most women. I even went so far as to suggest that men had a perfect right to have their own club and that perhaps the businesswomen who wished to join it should consider creating their own exclusive women's club where they could gather and talk about womanly things, out of earshot of insensitive, loutish men. However, I soon learned that I knew nothing of the feelings and genuine business concerns of women.

In actuality, this lady wanted to join a man's club because she wanted to be more successful in business. At that time, men operated and controlled the majority of businesses, (and the Government) and it was no coincidence that most of them belonged to this exclusive men's club. The power brokers of the community routinely got together in that place to talk about the Nation's business every day. They made multi-million dollar deals there and they hired some of their top executives from the ranks of its members. The Premier and many of his Government's ministers were members, which made it seem as though the entire province of British Columbia was essentially in the hands of the men's club. My lady friend knew what went on behind those old, stone walls and she wanted a piece of it. She wanted to take her rightful place at the table and get in on the power and glory of big business. She knew that as long as men could exclude women from what essentially amounted to an exclusive *business* club, women could not advance into the upper hierarchy of corporate culture. If they could not do business with men in the place where men preferred to do business, women would never become equal. When she spoke of fairness and equality, she was not speaking about women wanting to do manly things...she was speaking about the right of women to involve themselves in business on an equal footing with men. She felt that men were hoarding all of the power and money of the country behind those massive hardwood doors. I listened to her concerns intently and at the end of it, I had to agree that she was making a valid and important point. She wasn't complaining about men, she was complaining about being excluded from business opportunities. Ultimately a happy ending occurred...some years later that bastion of manly prowess finally allowed women full membership and today it stands as an example of just how powerful women really are. It seems that almost every major North American community has a clubhouse for business people. In the past they were virtually all exclusive to men. Now, most of the clubs are fully integrated. Men have grudgingly conceded their leather chairs and cigar smoke to the softer side of humanity. They don't all approve of what has happened, but in time it will become *just the way it is*...and the evolution of business will be complete.

In the community where I grew up, the Rotary Club was the organization of choice for businessmen. As a young businessman I knew the Rotary Club to be yet another exclusive men's organization. I was a little confused by that because the club did not own a building and generally had its meetings in hotel banquet rooms. Hence, membership did not involve passing through a check-in at the doors of the clubhouse and there were no leather chairs or cigars. Its membership included business people, loggers, sawmill workers, and salesmen. The only real qualifier for membership seemed to be that you must not be a woman. Despite that, Rotary clubs were known to do wonderful charitable things for their communities and they operated with integrity and noble purpose...all-in-all a great organization.

The most respected members of the community belonged to Rotary in the old days but they were all men. In the early nineties the unthinkable happened! The Rotary Club, on a universal level, was considering allowing women to join its ranks and become full members alongside men. They would be allowed to attend meetings, eat with men, work on projects with men and socialize with men. *"What's wrong with that?"* you might ask. It is a service club after all and it exists to do good work in its communities. Business people go there to meet and socialize with other business people in order to make contacts for future business opportunities and some just go there to enjoy a lecture from a guest speaker. Why would women be excluded from such innocuous activities? This is another example of evolution. Men were the power behind all business and when they decided to get together and start the Rotary club there would have been no reason to invite women in. Rotary started decades ago and at that time there were very few women actively involved in the business world. Contrary to the *women's lib* view, they were not excluded because male chauvinists rejected them…they were excluded because there were no female business people to invite into a business club at the time. However, as the years passed, it became the accepted wisdom of its membership that it was indeed, an exclusive male club and when women tried to join, some men were annoyed, shocked, and dismayed. I had an older friend who was an active member of Rotary at the time women began their initiative to join it. I will never forget his words to me when he found out: *"Wayne, if they let women into Rotary, they will destroy it!"* He was deadly serious and he made the commitment that if women were allowed into *his* club, the travesty would be so complete that he would have no choice but to resign his membership. He and others like him fought valiantly against the introduction of women into *their* club but when the smoke of the protests cleared, women were seated at the Rotary table clutching their hard-won memberships in their soft, yet powerful hands. My friend and a few others actually did resign from Rotary, but for the most part; the remaining men cordially accepted women as members. To the amazement of a few, Rotary was not destroyed and it lives on today in its happily integrated format, still doing great work in its communities.

So far it looks like women are getting their way on the exclusivity front. Whenever women find something that men want to keep to themselves, they demand to be allowed entry. They have joined men's business clubs, men's service clubs and even men's health and fitness clubs. In gyms all over North America, men and women run on treadmills side by side and *spot* each other with barbells. However there is an element of discriminatory exclusivity that seems to sneak under the radar ever so often that has nothing to with the treachery of men. If you drive around almost any city in North America you will find some sort of a *women's only* health and fitness club. These places overtly and deliberately discriminate against men. If you walk into one of them with an abundance of testosterone, you will not be allowed to join. Apparently and inexplicably, women do not want complete integration. They want to be accepted on a non-discriminatory basis in every man's club but they also want to maintain the right to discriminate against men at exclusive women's clubs. That just doesn't seem fair, Ladies! Fortunately men have little or no interest at all in forcing their way into clubs and organizations that cater exclusively to women so the folks who run them have not had to face a lot of protests or accusations of gender bias from them. Although men do not want to join, and tend to say very little about this slight against manhood, it is a very real bone of contention. My discussions with men about *women's only* clubs have made it amply clear to me that some men think less of women because of those clubs and use them as a reason to keep the ladies down. By asking men to, *"Do as we say, not as we do,"* women have weakened their position. They have created the appearance that women want to have what men have at any cost, but are not willing to be fair and equal to men when they desire something of their own. This inequality inadvertently drives an invisible wedge between men and women by preventing full integration of the genders in modern society. Of course we cannot blame all of womankind for a few thousand *women's only* clubs. They are owned and operated by people who see exclusivity as a business opportunity. Please don't accuse the ladies who join these clubs of any wrongdoing either. The female members feel safe and secure there, just as the men who enjoyed their scotch and cigars in the now obsolete men's clubs felt safe and secure in their exclusivity. I am optimistic that discrimination will be eliminated at all levels in the near future and that both genders will share equally in the spoils of current and past gender wars. My fingers are crossed!

While we are talking about women wanting into the lair of men, we cannot overlook the desire of female media reporters who want to get into the locker rooms of male athletes after games. If you are wondering why this is a matter of interest, you should understand that historically, women were banned from men's locker rooms just as men are still generally banned from women's locker rooms. Due to lawsuits in the 1970's, later in the 1980's all four major men's professional sports mandated equal access to locker rooms. University sports teams were slower to adapt to this new age equality until well into the 1990's. Prior to that, women were harassed and physically thrown out of men's locker rooms on a regular basis. The reason for the ban of course, was that men tend to wander around naked, or in various stages of partial undress once they have removed their sweaty uniforms after a game. When they are completely naked, they shower, socialize, and occasionally drink champagne with each other in the nude. Some men display exhibitionistic tendencies whenever they can while others are simply naked because they want to have a shower. Regardless of what causes them to become naked, the fact remains that they are on display in all of their manly glory and it seems inappropriate to many folks that female reporters should be standing next to them, in front of them, or behind them with microphones or note pads in their hands. I for one am a little uncomfortable being naked in front of anyone, but if I was a professional athlete I would think that I would be downright ticked off if a woman shoved a microphone into my face while I was toweling off my naked butt. I would not be happy if it was a man with a microphone either, but if it was a woman, I am quite certain I would instantly experience a range of emotions including embarrassment, annoyance and anger. Again, some men are left wondering why female sports reporters feel the need or desire to interview sweaty, dirty, hairy, panting, nude men in the first place. Why can't they just leave that chore to other men? We men know what we look like and we are neither surprised nor offended by our own naked bodies. However, we do have certain insecurities about the size and placement of certain of our bodily characteristics. We would generally prefer not to display ourselves to women who are not our mates or lovers and we generally do not display our genitalia to anyone who is not a doctor, a nurse, or the mother of our children. In fact in many countries in the world, if we display our genitalia to someone other than those mentioned, we will be arrested and thrown in jail for indecent exposure. So, why is exposure of male genitalia to a female sports writer any different than exposure of genitalia to a bank teller while making a deposit? The answer is simply that one exposure situation meets the approval of the women involved and the other exposure situation does not. How confusing!

Women want into men's locker rooms at least partially because professional male athletics are considered by many to be another example of the ongoing male subjugation of women. Professional athletes play a key role in the perpetuation of the concept of male dominance in society. Many women would like to tear that wall of superiority down. Any female reporter who made it into the locker room was throwing down the gauntlet of equality while daring male athletes to pass through.

Male athletes are cultural icons that stand for male physical superiority and sexual prowess. The best athletes are looked upon with envy and hero worship just as the Gods of ancient Greece were. Like Achilles and Hercules, they seem invincible and they live lives of luxury. Wealth is not the only benefit of a strong throwing arm, however. Women of all shapes and sizes routinely seek out athletes as bedmates and potential spouses. Men whose testosterone is utilized to its maximum muscular benefit are often considered beautiful by female standards. Women have been known to weep at just the thought of being in the presence of one of these muscle bound heroes. The female screaming and crying that occurs when famous male athletes enter a gymnasium or a stadium has little to do with the game they play. It has more to do with hormones and reproduction. Narrow hips, tight butts, and big chests are indicative, in a primeval way, of superior hunting and gathering ability. Those big, athletic guys are quite naturally surrounded by an aura that suggests they will be able to protect their women from all danger and create a life free of strife. Some women simply adore athletes because of their physicality rather than due to any sort of emotional love. For some, getting into a locker room with a bunch of naked sportsmen is a dream come true. Ouch! Before the female sports writers of the world gang up on me, please understand that those women are few and far between. Most have another reason for wanting to interview naked men.

The fact of the matter is that the locker room is best place to get the best stories. The best opportunity for really good, candid, exclusive quotes and comments from athletes is immediately after a game…at that point the adrenalin is still running and the players are still *pumped* from a win or downtrodden by a loss.

When at their emotional best or worst, they are most likely to say something controversial or memorable. Eliminating women from the locker room prevented them from becoming world-class sports reporters. Next-day studio interviews did not provide the same sensationalism as live locker room interviews with champagne-soaked, deliriously happy quarterbacks, dressed only in wet towels or nothing at all. Fortunately that wrong has been righted but as is the case with exclusive clubs, total integration is not complete. Male reporters are still generally not allowed into the locker rooms of female athletes. The only professional sports I have been able to find in North America that allow men into women's locker rooms are women's basketball, soccer and golf. In those cases, women will only do interviews in the locker room fully clothed, usually in the same garb they played in. They only disrobe once the reporters have left the locker room. Again the double standard appears. Why is naked, athletic female skin hidden from view while male bits and pieces are not? Okay, I get it! Society wants it that way…for now…

The point I am trying to make is that when women demand equality but refuse to offer it in return as is the case with *women's only* health clubs and locker room reporting, they prevent themselves from taking an equal place in society. The decision to avoid complete integration weakens the female position and allows men an excuse to continue thinking of them as lesser citizens. Human beings are driven by a competitive spirit in most things they do. Men and women are similar in that area. Men really do *not* want to join *women's only* clubs, so in order to compete and win with women who approve of separate ladies clubs they will simply hold them back and keep them down in other areas of business and finance.

Only when there is no segregation or discrimination by either gender will complete equality be achieved. Let's face it; women and men have been competing with each other and trying to *get even* since the dawn of time. If you interpret the term *getting even* as it relates to the genders, it is really a synonym for equality. Being *even* is the same as being *equal*. One must assume that if everybody *got even* at the same time, the genders would be able to achieve complete equality in all things other than physiology and physicality...the things that attract the genders to each other for reproduction. However, the human competitive spirit seems to be destined to prevent men and women from truly *getting even*. In reality, people who try to *get even* don't really want to get even...they don't want equality...they want to *better* or *outdo* another person. Most importantly, they want to win. As long as men and women are competing and trying to outdo each other, there can be no winners and no equality may exist. The conundrum is, who will crack first? Which gender will be the first to stop competing with the other, thereby allowing full equality to rein over our world? There may be no answer to the question because if either of the genders stops competing and begins to capitulate, they may not be considered even or equal. Capitulation, after all is an indication of *giving up*, so many members of the conceding gender will feel cheated by their own kind. Instead of creating equality, they will have created another layer of inequality that will be the subject of more concern and strife in the future. Gender equality is truly a vicious circle.

Lately, women have been moving into an ever-increasing number of previously male-dominated roles. Ladies now dominate the ranks of realtors and insurance company employees to the point that it is tough to find a man in most real estate or insurance offices. It turns out that women have a perfectly normal level of sales skill and are quite capable of presenting a home or an insurance policy in such a way that it is attractive and desirable...even to men! Who knew? Who knew that women could be sales people? *They* did! All they needed was the opportunity to get out from under the kids, the laundry, and the stove long enough to try. It is commonly accepted that women are in fact better at selling houses because they offer a more sensitive, attached approach to the homes they show. It is also accepted that a traditional couple (man and woman) will not purchase a home unless the woman is satisfied with two important elements of it…the kitchen and bathroom. When a woman is doing the selling, she will make darned good and certain that those two elements are suitable to the lady of the family. A male sales person might tend to gloss over those elements of the home or make light of their deficiencies. For whatever the reason, women are taking control of the real estate industry and have all but wrenched it from the grasp of men. How many other industries will follow?

Women have even taken on that much-maligned profession, *used car sales.* Admittedly there are still more car salesmen than saleswomen, but their numbers are growing. Thanks to Hollywood, the typical impression we have of a car salesman is a guy with a bad fitting suit, a cigarette, slick hair, and an even slicker sales pitch. These guys are your worst nightmare because once they have you in their clutches they won't let go. They will try to force you into a car that you simply cannot afford and when you dare to object they will systematically break your will through a well-rehearsed series of insults, threats, and character assassination tactics. They create payment terms that are irresistible and they demand that you test-drive the little beauty because they know that once you get behind the wheel, you will fall in love and simply *have* to own it. Imagine my surprise when I walked onto a car lot recently and was greeted by a well groomed, well dressed, attractive young lady. She said, "Good afternoon sir. Is there anything here I can help you with?" Not only did she not fit the stereotypical appearance of a car salesman…she was *nice*! I asked her if she was in a fact a car salesman and she responded in the affirmative. Sensing my surprise, she said, "Oh I know, you don't see many women selling cars but I enjoy it." She explained that she had been working in the car lot office but when she came to the realization that she could make a lot more money by going out front and selling cars instead of doing the paperwork on them from behind the scenes, she asked her boss to allow her to try. She was being paid on a straight commission basis and although her income was inconsistent from one month to the next it was much more than she could have ever dreamed of making while working in the office. When you think about it, there is no reason that selling cars, houses, or anything else should be the exclusive domain of men. You don't need testosterone to show off products and arrange financing. Now that women have started branching out there is no stopping them. Men will soon be playing on a level field with women and when that happens they will have to survive by their wits rather than their manly strength.

And how about those lady firefighters? I would have guessed that if a male who works for the fire department is called a fireman, a female who works for the fire department should be called a firewoman. However, since we now have firemen and firewomen working together in many fire departments, it was necessary to eliminate gender-based monikers altogether and more correctly, call them all *firefighters*. Women won on two levels with that one. The title implies that not only are they in the fire business, but they have been promoted to the level of *fighters*! Gender equality is tricky when it comes to creating titles in equalized professions. On a serious note, there have been several recorded cases of sexual harassment of firewomen by their male counterparts in fire halls. As much as women want to be fire people and society wants equalization of genders, a lot of firemen are still not willing to accept women into their ranks. The phenomenon is very much like the aforementioned issue of allowing female reporters into the locker room. Let's face it guys, a fire hall free from feminine companionship is like a dream come true for most of us. The guys in a totally male fire hall can eat what they want, watch whatever television shows they want, play poker, wander around naked, leave the toilet seat up, and pass wind at will. As soon as women were introduced into that once-sacred male domain, firemen assumed that they must watch their language, remain fully clothed at all times, and be politically correct in all they do. Again, women felt the need to force themselves into a male dominated occupation that pays reasonably well, offers an opportunity to save lives, and allows them to contribute to society in a very meaningful way...and once again they have been rebuked because of their femaleness!

Due to the obvious differences between men and women, fire halls had to be renovated to accommodate female firefighters. Sleeping quarters and bathing areas had to be segregated. Communal showers and latrines were no longer acceptable...nor were open bunkrooms. Today we find that most fire halls are designed to accommodate both genders in relative comfort and privacy. Living together was only one of the problems that lady firefighters encountered. As you might have noticed, women are built differently than men and tend to be on average, smaller in stature. Because of that, the protective gear that men wear will not fit most of them. Helmets, jackets, pants, masks, gloves, and whatever they wear under those bulky fire suits had to be redesigned for the ladies in order to provide proper coverage and protection during fire-fighting situations.

Despite 20 years of legislative reform and subsequent litigation, it has been reported that 85 percent of female firefighters indicate that they are treated differently than men; 80 percent complain that they are issued ill-fitting equipment; 37 percent feel that they have been verbally abused, and 50 percent feel shunned or socially isolated. Fewer than 4 percent of the firefighters in the United States are in fact women and more than half of the paid fire departments in the U.S. have never hired a female firefighter. Keep in mind when reading these statistics that women represent about 47 percent of the U.S. civilian workforce. Keep in mind too that in other jobs requiring strength and stamina due to dirty or dangerous work such as drywall installation, logging, and welding, women represent about 17 percent of total workers. It has also been reported that approximately 50 percent of the women who apply to be firefighters pass the same physical ability tests that male applicants must undergo. So why are there so few female firefighters? There appears to be no good reason why there should not be an equal number of female and male firefighters other than gender bias and sexual prejudice. It appears that the fire departments and Governments of North America might be holding the ladies back.

Let's talk about *why* society, (as represented by fire officials and Governments) might want to prevent women from becoming firefighters. I think the answer is quite simple: *Women don't have enough testosterone!* Women are generally smaller and appear to be incapable of carrying the weight of hoses, ladders, and life saving equipment that are common on fire trucks. Not to mention the fact that any self-respecting man cannot imagine himself being carried down a hot, smoky stairwell by a fragile woman. *Perish the thought!* Some male firefighters also fear that because of their protective, hunter-gatherer nature, they might be forced into a position of protecting their female firefighter cohorts from harm while also attempting to put out fires and save civilian lives. (I have heard similar complaints from male law enforcement officers who fear that their female *crime fighting* partners might not be able to handle themselves during physical combat or critical life-saving situations). Firefighters are revered and loved by all. The 9-11, World Trade Centre crisis brought firefighters to a pinnacle of respect and well deserved honor heretofore unheard of. The courage and devotion to duty of the men and women who responded to that tragedy is beyond question. Currently men dominate the fire fighting business where workers are considered almost *"God-like"* and *"sexy"*. However, the barriers to feminine equality are being torn down one by one and I am sure we will see far more female firefighters on the job in the future.

In the course of my research for this book, I was fascinated to learn that even the Christian Church has its share of gender bias…quite a large share, in fact. One of the most hotly debated issues in the church today is the subject of women who wish to become ordained as pastors, priests and preachers. Some power brokers in the church interpret the Bible quite literally on the subject. They quote from **1 Timothy 2:11-12** which states, *"A woman should learn in quietness and full submission. I do not permit a woman to teach or to have authority over a man: she must be silent."* The Apostle Paul wrote that women should not serve in teaching roles and should not have any spiritual authority over men. Some churches interpret that this statement precludes women in the twenty first century from becoming pastors, priests or preachers. One argument to the Biblical reference is that Apostle Paul had no choice but to prevent women from teaching and leading spiritually because at the time the Bible was written, women were not allowed any education at all and therefore would be completely incapable of teaching. To the women who wish to become ordained today, it probably seems a little unfair that an ancient quotation that was written in a time when women had about the same value to men as camels and sheep should prevent them from doing good work in modern times. Many dogmatic religious leaders however, maintain the belief that God intended men, and men alone to set the example for spiritual leadership for the world. In their minds it was God's plan to keep women out of the ministry and it is only God, not modern man, who will prevent women from being ordained. Case closed!

Over the past few decades, there has been a contingent of women in the Catholic Church who would like to become fully ordained priests. The Catholic Church has indicated however that it has no right to admit women to the priesthood. Rather than saying that the *Church* will not admit women, they indicate that the Church has *no right* to admit women and therefore the case has been closed again.

Interestingly, various interpretations also indicate that it is okay for women to teach other women and children...they just can't teach or lead men! Let's have a look at that Biblical quotation again, and this time, try to forget that it is in the Bible: *"A woman should learn in quietness and full submission. I do not permit a woman to teach or to have authority over a man: she must be silent."* My goodness! If a prominent, male businessman or politician made that statement publicly in the twenty first century, he would be chastised, censured, and scorned into oblivion! I would expect every newsperson in the world, female or male, to crucify him! Society does not want us to make statements of that nature and the world would prefer that men didn't even think such horrific and abusive thoughts. It seems that the church chooses not to follow society's rules, no matter how righteous when those rules run contrary to religious dogma.

It is not my intention with this book to be disrespectful of any aspect of Christianity. I am not qualified to make judgment calls about any religion. My intention with this information is to point out that women are facing a lengthy journey before they can overcome all of the history that got them to where they are today. There are many roadblocks to full equality and it is wise to be aware of as many of them as possible before setting out on that road. In the case of religion, some Churches have now admitted women to the ministry and perhaps more will follow with the passage of time.

Now let's return to sports but this time let's talk about female athletes. We hear about famous female racecar drivers, fabulous lady tennis players and great feminine golfers in the sports news every day. These ladies rival their male counterparts in popularity and are even beginning to overtake the lads in the area of pay scales. However, it has been a long, uphill climb for them. Golf, for example has always labored under the yoke of gender discrimination and in some cases it still does.

Popular chauvinistic mythology indicates that the word, **golf** is an acronym for the following negative phrase: ***"Gentlemen Only; Ladies Forbidden"***. I am pleased to say that deeper research has proven that not only is the origin of the word, *golf* in the English language a mystery, but there is no solid evidence to indicate that it has anything to do with ladies being forbidden to play the game. It is thought that the word may have come to the English language from Holland since the Dutch word; **Kolf** is a generic term for a stick or club used in a number of games similar to tennis, croquet and hockey. Linguistic researchers are not completely confident of that origin either, but they are quite certain that ***"Gentlemen Only; Ladies Forbidden"*** is not the origin of **any** word in the English language. Nevertheless, a lot of male golfers love to explain that definition of the word, *golf* to their golfing buddies as they roar around the fairways on their little white carts. Most men laugh uproariously when hearing for the first time that the origin of the name of their favorite game might actually be an acronym for discrimination against women. I think it actually fills some men with pride that their game is so decidedly the stronghold of men that even the name of it is rooted in male dominance.

Various golf clubs around the world blatantly discriminate against women by simply not allowing them to play on their courses. The really *big money* golf tournaments are male-only tournaments and even the name of one of the most prestigious tournaments; **"The Masters"** suggests male dominance. If, **The Masters** wanted to become an equal opportunity tournament and allow women to play, they might have to change the name to **The Masters and Mistresses** tournament! That would be an accurate name but it might not be considered politically correct. Oh by the way, have you ever noticed that on the male pro-tour the men always wear long pants, no matter how hot and muggy it is? Conversely, on the female pro-tour, *short-shorts, mini-skirts,* and *mini-skorts* are common. I don't think I need to say anything more about that.

Some golf courses that are not openly discriminatory will book *ladies days* and lady's golf tournaments on days and during times that are less appealing or advantageous...saving those good dates and times for men. Personally I think that women are buying-in and perpetrating male chauvinism when they agree to play golf on *ladies days* in the first place. It's just a game of hitting a little ball and chasing it around a lawn, for goodness sake! Why should there be days for women and days for men? I don't get it!

Another thing I don't get about golf is *ladies tees.* For my non-golfing readers: the spot where one tees-off, (or hits the initial shot on each of the eighteen holes or fairways), is generally referred to as the *tee.* Ladies tees are set much closer to the green, (where the hole is) than the men's tees. Hence the game is made easier for women since they don't have to hit the ball as far or cover as much ground as the men. When I play golf with a woman and she beats me while playing from the ladies tees, I have to admit I feel a little cheated. But, I only feel cheated for a brief moment because I would rather poke myself with bloody, dull fishhooks for four hours, than play eighteen holes of golf for the same amount of time. As you might have guessed, I am not much of a golfer, which is probably the primary reason I have trouble understanding why the game has played such a large part in the women's equality movement at all. By the way, note the spelling of *ladies tees* and *ladies days*. If the day or the tee is actually exclusively for the ladies, it should be spelled in the possessive form, "*Lady's tees* or *Lady's days*." *Ladies*, however is a common spelling on many scorecards and tee marker signs. Is that just another conspiracy to prevent women from owning any part of the game, or is it just bad spelling by male golfers?

I used to golf with a male friend who had quite a foul temper when things did not go his way…and nowhere was his temper tested more often than on the golf course. It was not unusual to see him yelling, swearing, and actually throwing his clubs into the rough, (bushes, trees, and long grass are called *the rough* in golf lingo). He was a bit like a cartoon character, stomping around while stringing many four-letter words and multiple-syllabic expletives together that had never been strung together before. On one occasion after four angry strokes, it soon became clear that he was completely incapable of driving his ball out of the woods and onto the green. After each swing he would throw his hands over his head and *duck* down to avoid being struck by his annoyingly errant golf ball. The ball would launch off his nine iron as intended, each time almost immediately striking the nearest tree and then bouncing back to another tree, and another, until finally coming to rest very near where it started. It was kind of like watching a huge, real life, pinball game. Finally, my friend became so angry that he actually took a violently hard swing at a completely innocent pine tree, wrapping the club completely around it. He then stomped back onto the fairway, threw a brand new ball on the grass, and exclaimed loudly, *"I give up, I'll take the @#$& %^ stroke!"* Many men reading this will identify with this story and are probably smiling and nodding with empathetic understanding right now. I ask you though, *"Have you ever seen a woman acting in such a fashion on the golf course?"* I never have. Out of curiosity, I asked one of my female golfer friends if she had ever witnessed a lady golfer screaming expletives while wrapping a golf club around a tree. She was dead certain that she had never seen such a thing, and also she had never heard tell of anything even remotely like it...*the difference between men and women rears its ugly head again!* Women are kind and gentle by nature and prefer either to simply accept the fact that they have difficulty with certain elements of the game, or refuse to accept defeat. When the latter happens they will quietly and confidently try and try again until victorious over the little white ball. They spend a lot of valuable time thinking the process through while attempting to create the perfect physical dynamic to launch the dreaded white orb off to one of its eighteen temporary resting spots. Men on the other hand will march up to the ball and flail away at it with obvious rage until it launches itself into the air. Hmmm...I guess that is why they have ladies days...it is almost a totally different game for them.

I am sure you will agree that men would prefer to watch other men golf because they can actually feel the adrenalin rush and an increase in blood pressure when a big-name male golfer lobs a ball into the rough. However, they have trouble identifying with female golfers and find little joy in watching them stroking a ball nicely around a course. If the lady's *or ladies* professional golf circuit wants to enjoy the prominence that the male version has, the ladies might have to curse a little more and make more of a spectacle of themselves. Professional sports are really just entertainment after all and if the players are entertaining, they quite naturally enjoy greater success. Ladies, if you do a little more stomping and swearing you might end up with more fans than the men before you know it.

Purses, or the winnings that professional athletes are paid are generally lower for women than men as well. Given that the sponsors of sporting events are generally promoting their businesses at these events, they want to put the lion's share of their money in the places where the largest number of people will be watching. Unfortunately for the ladies, male sports tend to draw a larger audience than female sports. Sponsorship dollars are based on the potential for increased sales of products and services to sports viewers, so anyone who wants to sell a lot of stuff would be wise to advertise his or her stuff during male sporting events. Unfortunately, that leaves very few sponsorship dollars available for women's sporting events and for the women who play in those events. Is that wrong? I guess it depends on whether you are a woman, a man, or an advertiser. Each will have a separate and distinct point of view.

Clearly, the reason that male sports draw the largest audience is because the majority of sports fans are men. Even men, who really don't like watching sports as a pastime will find themselves tuning into sports telecasts and watching the nightly sports news to find out who won, what the current scores are and who the star players are. It is a requirement and a covenant amongst men that they be knowledgeable in the area of professional sports. Any man who doesn't know the name and the statistics of the winning quarterback in the current year's Super Bowl game is considered a loser and a fool. He will be cast out of conventional male society and treated as a leper or worse, as a dork. He will be less than a man and an unsuitable conversation partner for others of his gender. Life is tough for men who are not obsessed with sports.

Of course, sports are important to men because of that old chestnut, *testosterone*...the motivator behind the overwhelming need to hunt, gather, and win. Sporting events often mimic fights, battles, and wars. In most games the intent is to win. Fortunately or unfortunately, depending on your perspective, in order to win, someone must lose. The essence of human competition is the need to win and since it is not practical for men to be fighting, battling or warring all the time, they created sports where a win could be had with relatively few injuries and hardly ever a death...although deaths do occasionally occur in most of the manly arts. In fact, the more brutal a game is, the more men are satisfied by it. Hits, injuries, blood and gore are the stuff that big-money professional sports are made of. Show me an injured player and I will show you two heroes...the guy who got hurt and the guy who laid the hurting on him. Of course, there are rules to these things and when someone gets hurt viewers are only happy if the rules were followed. In boxing, punches must be above the belt, (punching the head until the brain is dislodged from the cranial cavity is okay though). In hockey you can smash someone's head into the boards or the glass with great gusto, potentially causing permanent injury or paralysis, but if your stick comes up a little high and touches an opposing player's shoulder, you will receive a penalty. In football, you can run as fast as possible at an opposing player, grab him by any body part you can get your hands on, and throw him to the ground like a two hundred and fifty pound sack of potatoes, but if you raise your fist to the same guy you will be sent off the field. I must ask,

Ladies, *"Do you really want to take part in those sports and all of that violence?"* Frankly, as a normal red-blooded male, I hope not.

The various women's movements around the world are unhappy that women are not paid as much as men. However, it is not only men who are letting women down on sports equality…women too, are at fault. If women want to make as much as men in various sporting events, they need to encourage more ladies to watch them. If women boycotted male events and spent all of their time and discretionary income supporting female sports, they might be able to create a level playing field. Women do, after all, represent approximately fifty percent of the total population of earth and with that kind of a fan base they should be able to create substantially more revenue for their sporting sisters. However, I suspect that the majority of women reading this generally pay very little attention to female **or** male sporting events. They simply do not have the raucous enthusiasm for sports that men do. Because of that, it will be a very long time before equality will be allowed to rein on the fields, pitches, diamonds, rings, and courts of the world.

There is some hope for women in professional sports however. Racecars are now being built so that they do not require brute strength to be driven. Because of that, women can quite easily compete with men for the same purses. In reality, golf is more a game of finesse than strength. Because of that, compelling female golfers are inching ladies golf to the forefront of professional sports. Women have taken tennis by storm and the best of them are not only being paid on par with men, but they are also attracting more and more male viewers to ladies tennis with each passing day. The sports-women that make it to the top are the very best in their field and even testosterone-laden, armchair athletes can't resist the draw of their skill and charm.

However, many sports such as football, soccer, hockey, boxing and basketball will be very difficult for women to dominate. Even other women will turn away from female hockey players dropping their gloves and fist fighting at centre ice; they do not want to see a one hundred and thirty pound female football line backer tackling a beautiful, feminine quarterback; and they will avoid watching two ladies lacing up boxing gloves and punching each other into blood-soaked unconsciousness. These sports are suitable for big, burly hunter-gatherers…but not for the mothers of our children. My apologies are officially going out to the women's rights groups of the world right now, but I am afraid that much effort and energy is being wasted on these things. Some sports and some jobs are better left to the gender that can best handle the activities required to create the best result. Come on Ladies, you know I am right!

As I close this chapter, I want to say that I truly appreciate the efforts of women as they attempt to gain a foothold in male dominated occupations and activities. When a job is suitable to a woman I like to see a woman doing it. However, just as men are generally dreadful at most female dominated occupations and activities, there are some activities and occupations that are just not suitable to women! I think we should all be okay with that. I will support women when I think it is the right thing to do and as a free citizen, when asked, I will not support women (or men) in occupations and activities they simply cannot practically and effectively do. My goal with this book is not to criticize or pass judgment on either gender. It is instead to point out the challenges that men and women face together in the twenty first century.

Have you noticed that
women make the best mothers?

CHAPTER 6
Women as Mothers
and Daughters

As Max McMaster and Ron Johnson entered the clubhouse after their round of golf, they were surprised to see Max's mother seated at a table on the sundeck with some of her golfing friends. "Hey Mom, I didn't expect to see you here on Men's day!" Max exclaimed with delight. Max's Mom stood up and kissed Max on the cheek when he and Ron approached the table.

"You guys don't own the course you know! The girls and I just came out here for a quick bite to eat. Besides, we like to sit here and watch the men flailing when they try to kill the ball on the first tee!" she laughed.

"Well frankly, Mom I think having a bunch of women sitting here watching them probably makes a lot of the guys nervous. It's no wonder they miss a few shots." Max said with a serious tone.

"Yes, I suppose so, Maxy…that's what makes it so much fun!" she retorted.

The name 'Maxy' was always a little embarrassing for Max and his Mom knew it. Whenever Mary McMaster wanted to chide her son or let him know who was in charge of the family, she called him, 'Maxy". "Jeez, Mom I wish you wouldn't call me that in front of Ron and your friends!" he pleaded.

Ron could no longer control himself. "I love it, Man! Maxy! Ha Ha! Hey Maxy…let's go for a soda pop! Hee Hee, Maxy, I love it!!!"

"Oh for God's sake, Ron, control yourself! It isn't that funny!" Max scolded.

Mary put her hand over her mouth to stifle the laughter that was involuntarily coming out of her. Even though Max was forty-five years old, she still found it hilariously cute when he became embarrassed because of her. He was her only child and the apple of her eye but she had an infectious sense of humor that kept Max on his toes throughout his life. It was his mother's sense of humor that carried them through the death of his father and a lifetime of relative hardship. It was his mother's care and child rearing skills that gave him the determination and courage to graduate college and go on to become a successful, respected businessman. Max loved his mother and there was nothing she could say or do to shake his faith in her or his devotion to her.

After a bit more good-natured bantering, it became obvious that the ladies were anxious to get back to their conversation with Mary so she sat back down at the table to rejoin them. Max leaned over and kissed his mother on the cheek before the two men excused themselves and walked out to the parking lot for the short drive home.

As they exited onto the freeway, Ron said "You sure do have a great relationship with your Mom, Max."

"Yah…I guess growing up without a father and spending so much time with her created a pretty strong bond. But, you know something, Ron it also gave me a respect for women in general. My mom is not the only intelligent, strong woman in the world, you know. Beyond the obvious physical differences, women can do anything that men can, and it ticks me off a little that they are held back in business so often," Max said with conviction.

Ron gave his friend's statement serious thought before asking, "So do you think women will ever take over the business world?"

"Ha Ha! Well that's a leading question if ever I heard one!" Max laughed.

"Seriously, Max, what do you think the future is for women in business?" Ron pressed.

Max looked over at his friend in the passenger seat with a smile as he thought about his answer, "No, I don't think they will ever take over completely. I think they should and probably will, take over fifty percent of the top jobs. I mean, what the heck, the world is fifty percent women and fifty percent men. Why shouldn't they control fifty percent of everything?"

Ron's face took on a serious look as he responded softly, "The way the world is going, you might be right, Max. I wonder that will be like…Do you think you will ever see a female president at Maleo Industries? "

"You know something? There is this one lady that works for us who is setting the world on fire. Her name is Debbie Wilson and she was just transferred out of my region and into a senior VP job in head office. Now, there is a woman who doesn't even seem to know that there is any gender bias in business at all. She just keeps rockin' and rollin' her way to the top. She could be my boss one day." Max said reflectively.

"And I suppose you are okay with that?" Ron asked.

"Yup, I am," Max, answered confidently. "I trained her and I recommended her for the job. She is great at what she does and I would be proud to work for her!"

"You are an amazing guy," Ron said respectfully as Max's car pulled into his driveway.

Women who take child rearing seriously can have a huge effect on the lives of their children. The effect they have on their son's is powerful and undeniable…even though most boys will deny it when asked!

****

I have always had a great respect for women. Perhaps one of the strongest reasons for that is like most men I always felt a great bond with my mother. As a child, my mom kissed away the tears when I fell on the sidewalk and skinned my knee; she helped me with my homework when I had no idea how to add and subtract or even how to spell the words, *add* and *subtract*; she taught me how to tie my shoes (that was really quite tricky for me); and believe it or not she taught me how to cook, sew on a sewing machine, and run the vacuum cleaner. She gave me all of the basic life skills that I needed to get through childhood and adolescence and I still carry those skills with me to this very day.

While Mom was teaching me simple skills like tying my shoes and how to make bread dough, she was teaching me something else...she was teaching me to TRY. She was teaching me the value of effort. Mom taught me that no matter how difficult it was to tie my shoes almost everyone on earth knew how to do it so eventually, as long as I kept trying, I would know how to do it too. She taught me that if the bread dough collapsed while it was rising, it would not make good bread, but flour and yeast were cheap so all I had to do was repeat the steps in the recipe until it worked out. Most importantly, she taught me how sweet the fruits of my own, personal labor really could be. Anyone could go to the grocery store and buy bread. *Store-bought* bread is really quite tasteless and lifeless but it will suffice in a peanut butter sandwich. However, there is nothing like the taste of a slice of bread that is still warm from the oven with a bit of beautiful yellow butter melting across the face of it. Even without the butter it makes a wonderful treat. Just the aroma of bread baking is worth the mess and frustration of making the dough and waiting for it to rise. I learned from helping my mom in the kitchen that everything was possible and that if I tried very hard, there was a good chance that I could succeed at anything. Oh, and for those of you who have never made bread dough, you can use the same dough to make wonderful, fluffy donuts. You must be careful because they have to be deep fried, and hot vegetable oil is dangerous stuff. The risk is worth it though because when you pour the liquid icing sugar over those piping-hot, golden circles and pop them in your mouth, it is a like a little bit of heaven. The sense of accomplishment that comes from making and eating donuts is like none other. When you feel the warmth and taste the love you put into them for yourself, you will know what I mean. I think everyone should be fortunate enough to have the opportunity to make donuts with their mothers!

The sewing machine and vacuum cleaner expertise that I mentioned earlier might seem like odd learning choices for a hairy, testosterone-laden male, but there is a perfectly logical explanation. My father was a very *handy* guy who was always fixing things. In fact, when I was a child, it seemed as though he knew how to do almost everything *except* cooking, sewing, and cleaning. When I spent time with him on weekends he was usually busy working on the car, working on the house, or fixing something that was broken. I loved to watch him fix things and it always amazed me that almost any machine that had stopped working could magically come back to life with just the touch of his hands, the twist of his greasy old screwdriver, and a few well placed curse words. As a tribute to my Dad I still like to curse when I fix things. Even if it is an easy fix, I still like to call inanimate metal and plastic machines *sons of bitches* when I have repaired them and they are back working as intended. It just seems right for me to insult a machine that has let me down when victory over its once-lifeless corpse is mine. I have much nastier words for machines that refuse to allow me to fix them…but that is for another book. The point of all this is that I was lucky enough to have two parents who enjoyed teaching me how to do things. Thanks to Mom and Dad, when I came to the conclusion that I wanted to write my first book, despite the inherent challenges in writing an entire book, I just kept trying until I had enough words down in the right order to actually qualify as a book...that was four books ago and now I find the writing of books relatively easy when compared to the other things I do in the course of my life. Had I not learned the skill of *trying* from my mom I don't know if I would have gotten through the first one.

Because my mom generally did not work outside of the home, my dad supported the entire family on his solitary income and he had to work very hard to make ends meet. Salaries were low in the 1950's and we did not have a lot of money for luxuries. Because he was generally away working during the day and sometimes at night, I spent a lot of time with my mother. When I wasn't watching my dad fix things, I was watching my mom work. She worked at home all the time. She never stopped working except when she slept. I recall that she even made the shirts that I wore to school. They were fine enough shirts; just like any you would buy at Sears, and she often let me pick out the fabric she used. I sometimes had a twinge of envy when my friends showed up at school with the latest, stylish *store-bought* shirts but I beamed with pride when my friends marveled at the fact that my mom actually knew how to make an entire shirt. You see, even in the 50's most moms just fixed rips and tears in shirts. Hardly anybody knew how to make a shirt from scratch. That made my mom special...and that made me proud.

Watching my mom hunched over her sewing machine, pushing the material ever forward as its tiny motor whirred and rumbled, I could not help but want to try some sewing myself. Finally, one day my mom gave me some scraps of material and showed me how to sew them together. Then she showed me how to load the bobbin and how to string the thread through the various mechanisms that make it all work. The greatest thing was the buttonhole attachment. That strange looking thing would magically create the shape of a buttonhole and then all that had to be done was to pierce the material with a pair of scissors and suddenly there it was…a professional looking buttonhole. That might sound a little trite or insignificant but when you are a young man making a buttonhole for the first time, it is like magic. I found out quickly, that sewing was actually very difficult. If you push the material too fast the needle will jam. If you push the pedal too hard, the machine will run too fast and again the needle will jam or break. The needle itself had to be sharp, (so that it would not jam on its own) and had to be replaced from time to time. My mom knew instinctively the maximum thickness that the machine would handle, when the needle needed replacing, and intuitively she knew which jobs could be done on the machine and which had to be done by hand. She knew everything there was to know about sewing and as she was teaching me, I came to the realization that she was a very smart person with the same intuitive abilities and desire for accomplishment that were so evident in my dad. She was a woman though, and despite whatever skills and natural intelligence they might have had, women in the 1950's knew their primary role in life was as wife and mother. Women knew that the most important thing they could do was to be at home looking after the family while the dads were out making the money they needed to live on. I believe that families in those days, (true nuclear families) created a much better environment for child rearing than families in the twenty first century with two career oriented parents.

As a child, while learning how to fix things instead of replacing them and while learning how to cook, clean and sew, I was really learning self-sufficiency and independence. Today as a *fifty-something* man, I am still not afraid to try. The years have taught me what I am good at and what I am not, but I still want to learn new things and I still try to fix everything that breaks before I throw it out. I still do some vacuuming and I still do a lot of cooking. I must admit that my sewing skills have atrophied, but I think if I wanted to take sewing up again, it would be like riding a bike. Perhaps when I am completely retired I will start making my own shirts…even if just for the thrill of doing it. This book is called, *"A Man on Women"* and one of the most important things that happened to me during my life is that a woman raised me. My dad taught me a lot of great stuff and actually started me off on a business career that spanned four decades, but my mother was the one who gave me my soul. She showed me who I really was and gave me the courage to be me. She is also the reason that I am writing this book…it is for her.

While mothers today are at work, where are their kids? Most of them are in school or some sort of facility. Those who are too young to be on their own usually end up in a daycare facility when they leave school for the day. Some are lucky enough to be looked after by grandmothers, but in many cases people who are mothers, but not their own mothers bring them up. They are known as daycare workers. Don't get me wrong…I admire daycare workers. I certainly would not have the patience to look after a bunch of children that were not mine all day, every day. However, I don't believe that it is possible for daycare workers to provide the same kind of nurturing and teaching that my mother did. They are detached from the souls of those children. It is just their *job* to look after children. They cannot muster up the same kind of passion for their child-clients as their mothers quite naturally do. Children who seem aimless and troubled are often products of dysfunctional families. Families that show no interest in the day to day goings on of the children can expect to have kids that are difficult, often challenged in some way, and probably prone to getting into trouble. They need their mother's guidance and loving care in order to mature into well-balanced, productive adults. I understand the realities of the twenty first century just as I understand that in order to make ends meet, it is necessary for mothers to take on full time jobs to provide twenty first century lifestyles for their families. I wonder though, how many mothers would choose to work if it was not a financial necessity. Many women work at *jobs* rather than *careers* and they only go to work each day for a paycheck rather than for idealism or accomplishment. Because of that, not only are they in a position of being unable to fulfill the passion that all women feel for child rearing; they are deprived of the passion for their work that many of their husbands feel. Their lives then, are not nearly as full as they would like them to be.

Motherhood is an honorable profession. The Matriarch of any family should be put on a pedestal and praised for her courage and drive. I will state quite loudly and with confidence whenever the subject comes up, that my wife raised my children. Sure, I taught them how to ride a bike and how to run the lawnmower but all of the tough things like toilet training, getting out of bed on time, and general discipline, were handled by my wife. I got to do the fun stuff like taking everyone on holidays and to the carnival. I played with the kids in the yard and I bought a boat so that they could learn to water ski while I did the driving. My part in child rearing was easy and fun. My wife readily and willfully took on the difficult parts of raising our kids and frankly she did a great job with them. My son and my daughter are now both honest, hard working, constructive members of society and I believe that if I had tried to raise them on my own, they would not have been as good as they are today. They know it too. Both of my kids have a very strong bond with their mother that is evident, visible, and as unshakeable as mine is with my Mom. My mother's values have carried on through two generations of Kehl's and I am very proud of that.

As much as I am passionate in my belief that mothers who stay home to raise their children are doing the right thing, I understand that my model is quite impossible for many people in the twenty first century. Finances and the need for elaborate and indulgent lifestyles as dictated by modern society and modern media have taken the place of good, old-fashioned family values. We may never see a return to universal, matriarchal child rearing, but we must always value the mother's place in society and allow her to spend as much time as possible with her kids. Let's face it, without mothers to have babies the world, as we know it would come to an end in a few short years. Because that wonderful responsibility can only be borne by women, they must have time away from work to bear children and nurture them. Anything less is a travesty and a tragedy. If I could change the world I would allow mothers to just be mothers, but in the meantime we will have to make the best of what we have by giving mothers as much leeway as we can to be great influences on their kids.

I think I have made my respect for women as mothers very clear, but how about women as daughters? I grew up with one brother only...no sisters in my life. The only women I have any real experience with are my mother, my grandmother, my wife and my daughter. I never knew my dad's mother but my mother's mother was a wonderful person. She had a sense of humor that would not quit and she was so intelligent that even my dad could not beat her in any sort of battle of wits or thought-based contest. She was the kind of granny that all grandmothers should be like...loving, kind, and generous. My mother was of course, her daughter and I believe that my great experiences with my mother were at least partially due to the great upbringing my mom had with my granny. Daughters are almost always the direct and deliberate product of their mothers. It seems imperative that mothers teach their daughters all of the right things. Because of the direct link that daughters have to their mothers, if Mom does something bad, you can bet that a daughter will follow in her footsteps. If she does something good the daughter might just do something great. Of course there are exceptions to the rule and I know that some mothers and daughters have nothing in common and don't get along at all. In many families I have come into contact with however, mothers and daughters are so similar that I only need to talk to one of them to know what the other one is thinking. Their thought processes, tonal inflection, and even their facial expressions are so much alike that it is often quite startling. Even when mothers and daughters don't get along, it is not because they are different...it is because they are the same. If one is difficult the other one is bound to be just as difficult. In those cases it works out best when they agree to disagree and move on to other more pleasant things, avoiding any potentially contentious topics.

I think the bond that mothers and daughters have is a result of their femaleness. Women are able to drop their guards, show vulnerability, and talk about things fathers and sons would never admit to. I guess it is time to mention our old friend, testosterone again. Even in families, competition exists and in most families it exists in men more so than in women. Women like to hug either gender, while men prefer to shake hands with men...even with their sons. Getting too close to another man is difficult for testosterone to tolerate. Women have no problem crying with only minor provocation. A man would rather cut out a vital organ than be caught with a tear in his eye. Again, that is a testosterone issue. Women begin having menstrual cycles as teenagers. At that point, moms become extremely important to daughters because only mothers can understand the hormonal changes and resulting mood swings that begin to occur. As I mentioned earlier in the book men don't want to know too much about reproductive cycles, let alone talk about them. Unless your father is a doctor you should always talk to your mother about monthly cycles and the miracle of birth. Those exclusively female commonalities bring women together, particularly if they are mothers and daughters. Men have no real involvement in reproduction other than the sex act and they certainly do not have any physiology that can come anywhere near the trauma of a monthly cycle, so because of nature they do not have as many reasons or opportunities to bond with their daughters. Mothers and daughters are special and they are capable of relationships we men can never imagine or understand. At this point fathers and daughters all over the world are protesting that their relationships are just as special as any matriarchal relationships and I agree that men have been known to have wonderful, powerful relationships with their daughters. The underlying reasons for those relationships are different though. Please read on...

I think because of my respect for my mother and that darned testosterone, I generally find myself feeling unusually protective toward my daughter. My little girl is a very intelligent, thoughtful, compassionate person who was almost always on the honor roll in high school. She has always had a multitude of friends and an embarrassment of admirers. She also had the honor of being selected as the valedictorian for her high school graduating class. Her graduation day was a tad traumatic for me, I must admit. As a man who has done a good deal of public speaking over the years, I know how nerve wracking and downright scary it is to stand in front of an audience and say...well...almost anything! Public speaking is the greatest fear known to mankind, so imagine how hard my heart must have been pounding as my little girl was announced as the valedictorian; imagine how my hands began to shake as I fumbled with the controls on the video camera when she stood up and began walking toward the lectern; and imagine how frightened I was for her when she cleared her throat, adjusted the microphone and launched into her speech. If it had been my son speaking, I would have leaned back in my chair, smiled at everyone around me, and laughed uproariously at any silly thing he might say with all of the confidence in the world. For my daughter however, I was filled with fear, trepidation and empathy. I wanted to run up to the stage and stand guard over her or help her out with her speech. I wanted everyone to laugh at every even slightly funny thing she said, and I wanted to rain down harm on anyone who didn't appreciate what she must have been going through. She did great! She did me proud and in my mind, everyone in the room knew that she was the best choice her school could have made for the speaking job. Although I can't recall a word of it, I know it was the best, darned speech I have ever heard in my life! And that is a father's love. You daughters might not see it, but us dads have more natural, intrinsic love for our little girls than you will ever know. Some of us dads might seem aloof or uncomfortable around girly subjects and girly problems, but deep inside there is an abiding and unflinching love that nothing on earth can tear asunder. We might seem overly manly and exclusively interested in manly things or the things your brothers are doing, but we are watching you very closely in case you stumble; in case you fall; in case you cry. We love you very much and we live to protect you.

Because every father feels overwhelmingly protective of his daughter, he generally cannot stand the thought of any man touching his little girl unless he is a doctor, dentist or hairdresser. We all believe our daughters will remain perennially virginal and we know they will not *fool around* with the boys and men they date. When our daughters become mothers themselves, we are actually able to eliminate from our minds the thought that they might have had sex in order to produce our grandchildren. We prefer rather to assume that since an immaculate conception was recorded in the Bible, a virgin birth is quite possible. Hey Dads, isn't it great that our daughters were lucky enough to have immaculate conceptions just like Mary did??? Daughters are future mothers and mothers created and perpetrated mankind. They deserve respect and they deserve everything their fathers, husbands and brothers are able to give them.

Here are some interesting and telling facts about mothers. Firstly there are approximately 2 billion mothers in the world. There are more than 82 million mothers in the United States. In the 1950's mothers had an average of 3.5 children each; in the eighteenth century it was 7 to 10 kids, and in the twenty first century it has reduced to an average of 2 children per mother. On the child-raising front, women average 7,300 diaper changes by a baby's second birthday; preschoolers require mom's attention every 4 minutes or 210 times a day; mothers do approximately 88% of all North American laundry which amounts to 330 loads of laundry and 5300 articles of clothing per mother each year. Despite the fact that there appears to be very little time left in a day for mothers to work outside of the home, 72 percent of all North American mothers with children have outside jobs to earn money to support the household. Those working mothers average a 13-hour workday when the outside work and homework are combined. I understand completely why mothers feel the need to work since the cost of raising a child from birth to age eighteen in North America is approximately $250,000.00...that is a quarter of a million dollar per child!

On a very positive note, the busiest telephone usage day of the year is Mother's Day. Surveys tell us that approximately 122 million calls to moms occur on that day. It seems that mothers are generally appreciated on Mother's Day since in addition to the phone calls, 50 percent of North American households give Mother's Day cards, which amounts to approximately 152 million cards annually.

Many mothers miss out on education and career opportunities due to maternity. Studies have proven that the highest birth rates occur amongst women with the lowest educational attainment. It naturally follows that those with less education will have less opportunity to acquire or advance into high paying jobs. American women with college degrees can be expected to have a total of 1.6 to 2 children. American women with no college diploma and up to 8 years of education can be expected to average 3.2 children; those with 9 to 11 years of education can expect 2.3 children; high school graduates with no college degree will have an average of 2.7 children. This explains why birth rates are dropping as more women become educated and take on more lucrative jobs.

Now that you have read my treatise on mothers and daughters you might have a better idea why I wrote this book. Think about some of the earlier chapters and consider whether or not the mothers of the world are getting a fair shake in a male dominated world. Optimistically, I believe there is a quiet but determined equality movement bubbling under the veneer of North American culture. I also believe that now is the time for men and women to start working a little harder at understanding and accepting the obvious differences between them while respecting each other's rightful place in society. With plummeting birth rates not likely to abate, the next generation of working men and women are going to have to work side by side to maintain their lifestyles and enjoy all the world has to offer. If women and men will honestly seek out, define, and attempt to understand their fair and effective roles in our world now, the next few generations will have a much easier time of it.

CHAPTER 7
Women and Sex

As the men of the Maleo executive filed into the boardroom on September eighteenth two thousand and eight they were accompanied by someone that no one would have expected during the budget meeting of nineteen eighty-five. The newest senior vice president of Maleo Industries, Debbie Wilson walked briskly and confidently to her usual spot immediately to the left of president, Bob Martin's chair.

Max McMaster deliberately sat right beside Debbie. They had maintained their friendship throughout the years and coincidentally they had both been promoted to senior vice president in the same year. Everyone in the room knew that when Bob Martin retired, one of them would replace him. "Hey Deb, how's it going?' Max McMaster asked genuinely.

"Just great, Max. Our numbers are through the roof and I think this budget meeting is going to be a piece of cake. This is a record year for Maleo!" she said excitedly.

"Yah, I know, but I was really wondering how things were going for you personally. I heard you were having some problems at home," Max said quietly. Drawing nearer to her he followed with, "Am I out of line?"

"No you aren't out of line, Max. I trust you more than anyone. Yes, Jordan and I have decided to separate," she whispered, her voice cracking. "Can we have a private chat after the meeting?"

"Absolutely, Deb" Max said with genuine concern.

When the meeting ended, Max and Debbie headed to Max's office for the discussion that both of them knew the distraught woman needed to have. When they were both seated at the conference table in the corner of the office, Max broke the ice by asking, "So, is this for real. Are you really splitting up with Jordan?"

"God, this is so hard to talk about!" Debbie exclaimed, breaking into tears. "I can't believe this is happening!"

Seeing that Debbie needed time to collect herself before she could speak again, Max sat silently for a while before speaking. "So do you want to talk about what happened or why it happened?" he finally asked.

Debbie looked up at Max, her mascara, mixed with salty tears running down her cheeks. "He's banging our next door neighbor, Bonnie Schmidt," she blurted out. The sound of her voice saying those words struck her as funny and amid the sobs came a smattering of laughter. "Ha Ha, Ha, Max…so what do you think about that?" she asked with a crooked, tear-soaked smile on her face.

Max, truly shocked, immediately responded with, "Jeez, Deb. I can't imagine that. You are one of the most attractive women I have ever met. Jordan was damned lucky to find you and even luckier when you married him! What kind of an idiot is he?" he asked, almost yelling.

"Well, you know that Bonnie's husband is away on business a lot and so am I. Apparently one night when we were both away, they decided to get together and have a barbeque at our house. Jordan tells me that they had a couple of bottles of wine and one thing led to the next and they ended up in bed…our bed!" She shouted though her tears.

Feeling genuine, heartfelt sympathy, Max blurted out "Oh crap, Deb, I feel sorry for you!"

After having gotten her secret out in the open, Debbie relaxed and sat back in her chair studying Max McMaster's face. "Well thanks for that, Max. I guess I have to accept that sex is sometimes a more powerful force than the bonds of marriage and that if I had been paying more attention to that, Jordan would never have strayed."

"*You aren't blaming yourself, are you Deb?*" *Max asked. "It doesn't seem fair that you should take the hit for the two of them having sex behind your back!*"

"*I know it doesn't seem fair, Max. In fact I can hardly believe that all of this is happening, but I always knew that Jordan was an attractive guy with a big sexual appetite and if I didn't keep him happy, it might cause me some grief. I have to say now though that I really thought that his love for me would overcome my inattentiveness...but obviously, I was mistaken,*" *she said matter-of-factly.*

"*It just seems so wrong,*" *Max, said sincerely.*

Becoming more resigned to her fate and the changes that were about occur in her life, Debbie took several tissues out of the box on Max's desk and wiped the tears and mascara from her face. She felt a genuine closeness with Max and needed to try to help him. "*Max, don't ever take your beautiful wife, Julie for granted or think that she doesn't need you. Women want their men to show their love just as men expect their wives to be good lovers. Sex and the closeness of physical love make women feel safe and secure. When Bonnie's husband stopped showing his love for her, the writing was on the wall...and I guess I did the same thing to Jordan. You don't have to make the same mistake as we did though, Max. Stay close to Julie and show her that you love her. You won't regret it.* "

"*I am sensing that you might know something I don't know, Debbie, and frankly it is making me a little nervous,*" *Max said suspiciously.*

"*Oh no, Max! It's nothing like that...I don't know anything about your home life, or Julie's...I just know that your travel schedule is as hectic as mine and if you are not careful, you could end up like me. That's all!*" *Bonnie explained.*

"*Okay, thanks for the advice, Deb. So is it possible for you and Jordan to reconcile?*" *Max asked.*

"*Nope. Jordan let me know in no uncertain terms that my life and his are going in two different directions and the extra-marital sex was just a symptom of a bigger problem. He is not interested in reconciling and as much as I would like to turn the clock back and start over, I think he is right. It's just too late," Debbie said with conviction.*

"That's a damned shame," Max said calmly.

With that, Debbie Wilson stood up, thanked Max for the talk and walked out of his office. Max continued to sit at the table alone for a few minutes, ruminating over what he had just heard.

Usually, Max McMaster would sit at his computer reviewing numbers and dissecting spreadsheets well into the early evening. That night he left the office at four o'clock and went home to spend some quality time planning a vacation with his wife, Julie.

Sex is one of the most powerful forces on earth and it regularly shows its influence in almost all facets of human life. If you seriously consider your own life you will soon come to the conclusion that you are confronted with at least one situation that involves sex, sexual innuendo, or sexually charged thoughts almost every day. Now, let's discover how men and women really feel about sex.

****

She's HOT! He's HOT! You hear these things coming out of the mouths of women and men everywhere these days. Some young ladies find almost everything *HOT.* Often when they appear intrigued or confused by something someone has said, they will blurt out, *"That's HOT!"* Now we have an entire generation of children and young adults saying *HOT!* Clearly the word *HOT* has taken on a new meaning in the twenty first century. From what I am able to understand, *HOT* is the new *SEXY.* The common definition of intense warmth has been broadened to include the natural warmth that a person feels when they are sexually attracted to another person. Sexual attractiveness is now measured by the degree of *HOTNESS* a person possesses.

Because sex is such an important element of human life, folks are even able to apply sexiness ratings to inanimate objects, social events, and simple commentary. Almost anything that is appealing in the twenty first century is considered *HOT*. So what does *HOT* really mean?

For both genders, hotness varies between individuals. Everyone seems to have a *type* they prefer. The closer a person is to their *type*, the hotter they are. You often hear people saying, he is not my type or she is just my type. *Types* are easily explained by the sciences of human evolution and physiology. Take oxytocin for example: Oxytocin is essentially one of the many hormones in our bodies that make us who we are. Men and women both carry oxytocin and although its true purpose is unclear, it increases in human bodies during the orgasms of both men and women and in the bodies of women during childbirth. Interestingly and inexplicably, oxytocin has been found to increase our levels of trust and create a higher level of connection or a bond with the people we have sex with. It also increases the level of connection that both men and women feel for their newborn children because when babies are born, mothers and fathers experience a surge of oxytocin. In addition to a more loving sexual experience, oxytocin has been found to counteract the natural stress hormones in our bodies, which of course allows us all to experience a pleasurable, and guilt free sexual experience along with an *afterglow* of relaxed bliss. Essentially, if a man or a woman feels a strong sexual attraction toward another human being, it will be accompanied by a surge of oxytocin that will work its magic to bond that person to their intended mate. People are considered *HOT* because of various elements of physical attractiveness, personality traits, status, wealth, and power, but most importantly, oxytocin.

It is believed that testosterone has the ability to reduce the effects of the oxytocin that surges through a male body, while the estrogen in women appears to enhance its effects. It is also believed that women have many more oxytocin receptors than men and are therefore more affected by it. Those two discoveries help to explain why men choose not to caress and cuddle after sex to the extent that many women would like. Once the oxytocin surge has abated, a man is ready move on to other things, while the woman is usually still in an oxytocin-induced mood for a romantic connection and continued bonding. So there you have it, Ladies; science has now uncovered the reason for the age-old image that men have of not being as romantic or caring as women. Their disinterest in post-sex cuddling has more to do with physiology than it does with insensitivity or a lack of passion. Keep in mind too, that the oxytocin surge is unconscious. It occurs in the autonomic nerve area of our brains where thoughts do not control actions, so it is not something we can turn on or off. It just is what it is. I am able to deduce from all of this that if one man is considered more romantic than another man during and after sex, it is not because he is more caring or compassionate…it is simply because his oxytocin surge level is greater than the other man.

Oxytocin is such a powerful attractant that people often get together and stay together because of sex rather than because of true love. When human beings have oxytocin surging through their bodies due to the anticipation of a sexual adventure, they become so enamored of the bliss they are feeling that they ignore any obvious personality issues that the other person might have. Men, who might be completely objectionable in every other way, are often forgiven because of their sexual prowess and the afterglow of bliss that their women feel toward them. Hence, oxytocin may be inadvertently responsible for millions of bad relationships all over the world. When people are falling in love, they must be cautious not to assume that the love they are feeling is sustainable. It may be just the temporary glow of an oxytocin surge. When other, more negative traits of their lovers begin to take prominence in a relationship, oxytocin surges will abate and the *loving glow* will disappear. At that point, love will diminish and the relationship will break down.

Chemicals that are common to all warm-blooded animals spur oxytocin on. Pheromones are airborne chemical molecules that travel between virtually all animals of the same species. Humans are loaded with pheromones and they have played a big part in male/female relationships throughout the evolution of mankind. Not only can pheromones cause us to experience a variety of emotional reactions, they are known to have a powerful impact on hormone levels, fertility and sexual stimulation. Essentially, pheromones are messengers that unconsciously give other people and animals an array of information about the attributes of our immune system, our level of aggressiveness, and even our level of sexual desire. We are all surrounded by an aura of our own pheromone molecules at all times.

Each pheromone molecule contains our own, unique chemical identity that is as different in each of us as our DNA. Although you are completely unaware of it, your sweat glands and your hair are sending out pheromone messenger molecules to the air around your body at all times. They are sensed and processed by two tiny organs inside our noses that ultimately send signals to our brains about the person whose pheromones we have come into contact with. When that happens, a message is sent to the hypothalamus area of the brain that controls our primitive emotions and reactions without regard for cognitive thought. When we experience an inexplicable positive or negative reaction toward another person it is probably due to the chemical signature of their pheromones.

The main pheromone emitting areas of the body are the groin, the armpits, and the nasal sulcus; that grooved area between the nose and mouth where men often grow moustaches. Your hair plays a part by trapping and holding pheromones when they are emitted from the sweat glands. It is believed that men and women kiss, embrace, dance closely and have oral sex as a method of getting as close as possible to the pheromone-rich areas of the body. Once they have sampled a good dose of their partner's pheromones they are in a better position to evaluate them as a potential mate. When your dog is sniffing or nuzzling you he or she is sensing your pheromones too. Puppies learn a lot about you when they sniff your scent.

As we learned earlier, a large part of human mating practice has to do with hunting and gathering by men and child bearing and rearing by women. Because the pheromone molecules of each person carries information on the immune system and sexual proclivity, primitive men and women were able to determine from unconscious pheromone processing whether their mate was likely to be healthy, immune from diseases, and likely to want sex often enough to create a large family. Human brains are still processing pheromone molecules in the same fashion they did for Neanderthal brains during prehistoric times. Then as now, if the pheromone molecules are putting out a desirable chemical message to the receiver, oxytocin levels will begin to rise and a relationship will be born.

Interestingly, because human beings enjoy sex more than almost anything else, the world of cosmetics marketing has created an entire industry based on pheromone enhanced perfumes and colognes that are engineered to increase the wearer's sexual attractiveness. The next time you are close to someone who *smells good* be careful that you are not being duped into a relationship with him or her by some bogus, bottled, pheromones they might have been dobbed on in the bathroom earlier that morning. On the other hand, if you feel the excitement has gone out of your relationship, you might try splashing on some pheromone-laced cologne to spice it up a bit.

DNA too, has a bearing on how women relate to men. Our DNA is essentially a nucleic acid that is responsible for transmitting hereditary characteristics and for the building of proteins in the body. It carries the memories of our ancestors. Each person's DNA is specific and unique to that person. DNA is best known for allowing the criminal justice system to identify bad guys beyond a shadow of a doubt. Forensic scientists are able to look at the DNA found in hair, blood, or tissue samples found at crime scenes and match it up exactly with the person it belongs to. It is the most revolutionary crime-fighting tool ever created. Believe it or not, it is also one of the main determinants in male/ female relationships.

The DNA imprinting of men is based on prehistoric values and judgments. Because of that, men are driven to relentless pursuit of activities that will allow them to provide for the women in their lives. Even in our modern world where gathering food and killing animals to survive is no longer necessary for most people, men will do everything they can to provide sustenance to their mates. In ancient times an abundance of food was a symbol of status and wealth. Things have not changed very much since those simpler times. Today, a man seldom feels the need to slay a wildebeest and triumphantly deliver the carcass to his mate. However, in the twenty first century a man will take his woman to an expensive restaurant as part of his obligatory display of strength and stature. With luck and some good pheromones, a gift of great food can get a man into the marriage bed with his intended mate, just as prehistoric hunting and gathering did. The more things change, the more they stay the same!

A man's DNA tells him that his first interest in any woman should be to have sex. In fact his DNA tells him that he should have sex as frequently as possible with as many mates as possible. Men generate millions of sperm every day and their DNA programming tells them that they should implant them into the wombs of many women so they can continuously repopulate the planet. Promiscuity is not only common in men; it is completely natural and should be expected. Women on the other hand have DNA programming that tells them to seek out protection, and commitment from one man at a time. Because of that fundamental difference between men and women, if a man wants to have sex with a woman, he would be wise to show her that he is reliable, available, and committed. Because women are conditioned to be able to control their sex drive, they don't have to flip their passion switch until they are certain that their man has the attributes and values that are necessary to satisfy their long term need for safety and security. There are of course, exceptions to the rules of mankind but ancestry is still controlling the actions of most modern women and men through DNA imprinting.

Because of ancestry, evolution, and DNA imprinting women often tend to favor aggressive males as mates. They want men who display power and courage because their primitive need for security and protection causes them to believe that aggressive men are much more likely to protect them and their children. A feeling of safety and security is an unconscious prerequisite for all women prior to offering up sex. Despite that need in women, men must realize that their aggression must be controlled and not offensive to the women they intend to mate with. Men should clearly and deliberately exhibit their desire for the women they pursue, but they must not be pushy, loud, or physically abusive. A modern woman wants a man to show her that he knows what he wants and is not afraid to go after it, while at the same time offering enough sensitivity to convince the woman that his aggression will not be directed toward her in a threatening or harmful way. Once an aggressive approach has gotten a man through the door, he must become nurturing and caring in order to convince his intended mate that he will care for and protect her and their children. Again, women do not cognitively consciously consider these things while dating, but those are the instincts that drive their feelings.

Let's look at some of the other *types* women like, starting with *the strong, silent types*. Those quiet but determined guys are attractive to some women because for them, a deliberate but less brash approach is better since it is not as threatening. Note that *weak, silent* men seldom have much luck with women. Strength is important to an active romantic life. Financial success is another modern indication of aggressiveness and power and it is a fact that wealthy men have much less difficulty attracting a mate then their less fortunate brethren. Women like intelligent men for the same reasons. Obvious intelligence is an indication to a modern women that a man will be capable of making a good living and therefore able to support and protect her family. Ladies tend to like funny men too. Because jokes are funniest when something is said that the listener has not heard before, or is said in a unique way that makes it funny, a good sense of humor is considered an indication of intelligence or exceptional knowledge. Of course it is also an indication of light heartedness which most people find calming and therefore appealing. Funny guys generally have less trouble finding a mate than serious, boring guys who prefer to talk about business and statistics rather than trying to make people laugh. The great thing about all of this is that when a man is outgoing, rich, intelligent, or funny, his aesthetic appearance or attractiveness will be of lesser importance to the women he meets. That is why you often see homely men with beautiful women. Women tend to look for powerful traits in men that indicate an ability to provide the security they quite naturally want and need. Attractiveness is much less important to them than it is for men whose primary interest in mating is for sex. For women, a man who can provide them with safety, security, and a good life is *HOT!* For men, the more sexually appealing a woman is, the better she will be as a mate. Many men feel that any beautiful woman with great lips, legs, breasts, and buttocks is *HOT!* However, because there are a limited number of women who fit that description every man will not end up with a sexually stunning mate. Those good looking ladies can pick and choose which men they mate with just as wealthy, intelligent men can. Life often seems unfair on a sexual attractiveness level but sadly, looks and a great body can never guarantee a great relationship for any length of time. For those people who are less appealing life can be very sad and lonely indeed. Out of desperation or pure loneliness, many people will choose to settle for someone who does not appeal to them on all levels of security or attractiveness. Those relationships often end in failure. On the other hand, any couple that is fortunate enough to bond on an emotional and intellectual level will push sex appeal to the back burner in short order and simply revel in each other's company. Those are the great long-term relationships that storybook romances are made of. Statistically, there is a man for every woman and a woman for every man. The trick is to match them up so that everybody has the right one.

Often we will find that normal, feminine women from good families are attracted to *bad boys.* Men who are involved in criminal activities, who get into a lot of fist fights, or who ride in motorcycle gang's hold an unusual fascination for some of the gentlest of females. Again, the power and aggressiveness exhibited by reprehensible behavior or involvement in dangerous activities tends to create a sense of security in the minds and hearts of some women. In addition to the need for protection, there is an element of adventure and excitement that goes along with hanging out with a *bad boy*. That phenomenon shows itself in the field of rock and roll music as well where even the shabbiest, unattractive, and emaciated rock stars have *groupies* banging down their doors for sex every night. For *groupies* it is less about the music and more about the potential for the protection and safety of being with a powerful, wealthy mate. Of course if the bad boy or rock star is attractive by modern, human standards, his chances of multiple bedmates increase dramatically. The significant down side to relationships with *bad boys* is that they usually don't last very long. Usually the *bad boy* will take up with one woman after another or he will direct his reprehensible behavior toward the woman who loves him, destroying her faith in him and bringing negativity to her life. Many a woman in those situations will become leery of future commitment to any man, thereby preventing herself from experiencing the joy of life with a good man.

Most warm-blooded animals perform courting rituals prior to having sex. Male gorillas for example will grunt, stomp and thrash around the jungle for up to five hours prior to a sexual encounter with a willing female. Human males tend to spend more time chatting up their intended mate than they do stomping and thrashing but the ultimate outcome is the same. In modern, western culture sexual courtship can be as short as a few minutes but all of the dynamics heretofore discussed will be activated during those minutes. Pheromones, oxytocin, DNA, ancestry, and evolution will all be involved in virtually every human sexual encounter, no matter how long or how short it is.

You might think that given the complexity and difficulty of male-female relationships, men and women would want to mate for life. However, it is a fact that the North American divorce rate is now verging on sixty percent. Hence, it follows that there are now more divorced people than married people on our continent. Interestingly, almost twice as many women as men file for divorce in North America. The reasons most often given by women for divorce include, but are not limited to, mental cruelty, neglect, emotional abuse, and abandonment. Abandonment can be described as either emotional or physical. Essentially all of these reasons, or *grounds* for divorce are based on the detachment of one mate from the other. All of the *grounds* mentioned here are based on the concept of a man avoiding a close, secure, emotional relationship with his wife. The evolution of male-female relationships has led us to the point that men may no longer just act as hunter-gatherers...they must now add *soul mate* to their list of manly duties. I am afraid that statistically, based on the divorce rate, most men are not up to the task of being a strong emotional partner to a woman for an extended period of time. It seems that we just cannot bring our testosterone-packed minds to an emotionally stimulating level for women on a regular and consistent basis. We would rather hunt and gather. We would rather play golf or beat other men at poker than talk to our wives about a nasty co-worker, a difficult monthly cycle, or a bratty teenager. We want to turn our minds off after work and just stare aimlessly at the television set. And speaking of the ubiquitous TV, we would rather watch a football game than a romantic comedy. We are different! If you want to stay married to your man, Ladies you might have to settle or compromise with his male needs and wants. And Gentlemen, you too must capitulate a little if you want to avoid the needless pain and expense of divorce. Find your feminine side and try to bring it out from time to time. Women tend to be very compassionate and flexible so if you try just a little harder to pay attention and satisfy your lady on every level, your efforts will be well rewarded. The bottom line for a successful marriage is open, honest communication. If you do not discuss with your mate the things that bother you about your relationship, you will soon become one of the sixty percent of North American people who ultimately lose the right to sleep in the same marriage bed for a lifetime.

It is interesting to note that only in recent centuries have the ideas of *love* and *fidelity* become part of the mating ritual. Still in various parts of the world, and in various religions, those concepts have become skewed to suit local traditions and customs. Because all the people on earth are Homo sapiens and therefore functionally the same, it is clear that the human brain can twist its DNA imprinting to suit the cultural pressures of the day. In other words, at this point in time North Americans have decided that if two people want to mate they should be in love and they should live together monogamously...free from sex with others of their species. That manner of living is not natural to most warm-blooded animals and it is specifically not natural to human beings. It is simply what has become culturally acceptable at this point in time. This helps to explain why so many marriages end in divorce. Even though society tells us that we should be exclusive to one mate, our natural DNA imprinting tells us otherwise. Our natural tendency is to leave our mates and find others in order to procreate. Hence, as society's rules change we are seeing more and more divorces. In addition to that, we are seeing a huge number of couples choosing not to marry but rather to live together outside of Holy wedlock. Perhaps in the future we will see a return to our ancient roots when marriage did not exist and people had no restrictions at all on who they mated with.

The next question one might ask is: "Do women actually like sex?" The answer is, "You're darned right they do!" They love it, but they love it differently and they are more particular about it than men are. As much as titillation and sexual fantasy are common to women, those thought processes are not as common to them as they are to men. I don't think there is any truly reliable statistic on how often each gender fantasizes about sex but researches are clear on the fact that females fantasize significantly less often than males. Of course, that is because it is a man's purpose in life to fertilize the eggs of many willing females while a woman's purpose is to receive sperm and produce children. Sex may actually be better for women due to their naturally longer oxytocin surges and their propensity for multiple orgasms. Women also take longer reaching orgasm than men…at least twice as long or much longer in many cases. That might be a good thing or a bad thing depending on the emotional sensitivity of the man. If he is willing to stay the course until his woman orgasms, her experience will be much more pleasurable than his, due to the duration of her rapture and her extended surge of oxytocin. Many more women than men have difficulty reaching orgasm during sexual intercourse, which helps to explain the twenty-first century's proliferation of female masturbation tools and toys. Just walk into any sex shop and you will find an incredible array of dildos, vibrators, prosthetic penises, and God knows what else. These stores, along with online suppliers are growing in numbers every day. That alone tells me that women enjoy sex very much. However, it appears that they don't enjoy it with men as much or as often as men enjoy it with them. Some women enjoy the safety and security of solitary masturbation without a man present to threaten or disappoint them. Others resort to masturbation because they are simply not having memorable or satisfactory sexual encounters with their mates. In many cases, they are having no sex at all. Remember that a woman prefers to choose a specific man and become confident in his ability to protect her and care for her children before offering sex. An average man on the other hand, generally masturbates often, but would much rather have sexual intercourse with a real, live woman...almost any woman...any time. Unfortunately for women, a man's primary goal is not to cause orgasms in his mates. It is instead to cause his own orgasms. If you want to stay married to, or partnered with, a particular woman for any length of time, Gentlemen you must learn to pay attention to your lover's sexual needs. If you fail to satisfy her time and time again, she will soon lose interest in you no matter how much enjoyment you are getting from her. And Ladies, if you are having trouble reaching orgasm or enjoying sex with your man, you need to tell him about it. Describe the problem and what he should do about. Men are smarter than they look and it is amazing how they can learn and adapt with a just a little instruction and encouragement.

No discussion of female sexuality would be complete without a mention of lesbianism. Let's get the most controversial stuff out of the way first! Despite what some people think, all major mental health organizations in North America have confirmed that homosexuality is not a mental disorder in any way, shape or form. Secondly, from a medical, psychiatric or physiological perspective it is neither an aberration nor a perversion. It is now considered to be normal and frankly, not something to worry about, (as heterosexuals tend to do). Homosexuality and bi-sexuality are common in the animal kingdom and it would be surprising if it were not common in humans. It is believed that ten percent of North American men and women are homosexuals, which makes it more prevalent than many heterosexuals would expect. Statistically, one in ten of your neighbors or co-workers could be gay! An interesting discovery that has come out of seemingly endless and exhaustive studies of human homosexuality is that women are less gender-specific in the area of titillation than men. When tested, heterosexual men tend to become aroused when exposed to scenes of men and women having sex or two women having sex with each other. They tend not to be aroused at all when exposed to scenes of two men having sex. Heterosexual women on the other hand, when tested proved to be aroused by male/female sex, female/female sex, and male/male sex. Clearly for women, titillation comes from being exposed to two or more human beings in the throes of sexual union regardless of gender. Women's minds seem to be more sexually liberal. That helps to explain the closeness that women feel for each other and the fact that women seldom shy away from a hug or a kiss from another woman. It might also help us understand why heterosexual women are quite comfortable with, and occasionally attracted to homosexual men. Gay men tend to be less threatening to women and those who appear quite feminine are so non-threatening that women often want to spend a good deal of time with them as friends or co-workers. The sexual choices of gay men are in no way repugnant to many women. Conversely, even though the sight or even the thought of two men kissing repels most men, they enjoy seeing two women kissing or having lesbian sex simply because their titillation factor is doubled at the sight of two women having sex. The truth of the matter, Ladies, is that when men see two women kissing or having sex, they immediately begin to fantasize about having sex with both of them at the same time. Although homosexuality is latent in ten percent of the population and evident from early childhood, it may often be hidden or withheld for much of a person's life. The feelings of homosexuality may ebb and flow with the tides of cultural and family pressures, but generally if someone has the predisposition to be a lesbian or a gay man, that latent need will ultimately emerge as a powerful force at some time in their life. Some folks act on it and some don't. From what I can understand, sex and love between lesbians is no different than sex and love between heterosexual couples except that the aggressiveness and dominance men bring to relationships is reduced or eliminated altogether.

Speaking of aggressive men, Ladies, if you want to be left alone by men on a romantic or sexual level, just let them know that you are a lesbian and have no desire to change. Some guys might try to talk you into changing, but most will be intimidated enough to simply back away and hunt down another prey. Finally, if you are a lesbian be okay with that and take heart in the fact that society is changing and cultural rules are evolving to allow homosexuality to exist as an accepted and common lifestyle choice.

Oh by the way…in case you were wondering what I find *HOT*…I find *HAPPINESS* very *HOT!* I find happy people very appealing and I wish every woman and man on earth could be happy all the time! Have you ever noticed the attention that happy people naturally get from others? Have you ever noticed how much more attractive smiling or laughing people are than angry or sad people? If you want to be more appealing, more attractive, and have more sex appeal, try smiling and laughing a lot more!

So there you have it…sex for women is much more complicated than a night on the town and a happy ending. It is so amazingly complex on a scientific level that it is easy to see why men and women have difficulty staying married or just getting along with each other at all. In order to be successful, much patience, effort, and understanding is required from both genders in every relationship. I am hoping that this information will help women and men better understand what is driving their relationship urges and challenges so that both can have more and better opportunities to co-exist in harmony.

CHAPTER 8
A Man on Women

It was January fifteenth, two thousand and ten when Bob Martin appeared before his board of directors to make an announcement that would change the course of history at Maleo Industries.

As he stood before the board of exalted business leaders who directed the operations of Maleo, Bob was unusually nervous. "Gentlemen, I have finally made the decision to retire from the company and take it easy for the rest of my life," he said in loud but uncertain tone. When it was out of his mouth, he felt a wave of euphoria wash over him such as he had never felt before. Suddenly he realized that all of the stress that he had been facing every day for most of his working life was behind him. Never again would he face the problems of management; never again would he be responsible for the success of the shareholders, or the lives of his employees. He was finally free. His whole life was before him and he was ready to live it to the fullest...his way!

Chairman, Hugh Braxton was the first to speak. "Well, before we start talking about business, I want you to know something, Bob; you have been a great leader at Maleo and you are one of the finest gentlemen I have ever known. Your contribution has been great and you will not soon be forgotten. There aren't many good men like you around and I don't suppose we will ever really replace you. I respect your decision though and we all knew that *this had to happen sometime. There…that's enough mushy stuff, now what the hell are we going to do about a replacement president?"*

One of the board members, Dave Kehler, spoke up, "Hey, Hugh, I have been keeping my eye on that Max McMaster for years now. He's always been a great manager and since he was moved up to senior VP, he has made some great strides in his division. I like him a lot. Why don't we give him a shot at president?"

Hugh Braxton looked at Bob Martin, "So what do you think, Bob? I know that Max has been one of your closest guys for a long time. Do you think he can cut it in the top job?"

Bob smiled and quickly looked around at the faces behind the boardroom table before speaking, "I already thought of him and I even asked him if he wanted the job."

"So don't keep us in suspense. What did he say?" Dave asked impatiently.

"He said no," Bob replied, still smiling.

"So, Bob, what's with the smile on your face? What are you not telling us?" Hugh Braxton asked.

Bob paused before speaking, "Well gentlemen, knowing that I might ask him to take over my job, Max was ready for me. He had a well-prepared report written on why he thought that although he could do the job, there was someone else in the Company who could do it better than him. After reading the report, I realized he was right."

"Okay, so who is it?" Dave Kehler asked.

"Yah, who is it?" Hugh Braxton echoed.

"It's Debbie Wilson!" Bob blurted out almost defiantly. After he said it, he sat back in his chair to survey the faces of the mostly grey haired males around the table. He assumed that the idea of putting a woman in charge would be thought of as such a radical concept that it would be immediately voted down. He was ready to defend his position and do battle to put Debbie into the job. However, he was delightfully surprised at what happened next.

"So, Dave, you have been doing a lot of talking today. What do you know about Debbie Wilson?" Hugh Braxton asked Dave Kehler.

"Well, she has been a shooting star in the Company and as much as I am disappointed that Max doesn't want it, I have to say that she is the best candidate. The world is changing and maybe it is time we changed with it. My vote is that we do it, dammit! In fact I will formally nominate her for the job!" Dave said enthusiastically.

"Okay, let's put it to a vote. Dave has nominated Debbie Wilson and I am seconding it…all in favor?" Hugh Braxton asked with anticipation.

Every hand in the room went up and with that, Debbie Wilson became the president of one of the largest corporations in North America. She would be the first to admit that she sacrificed her personal life to become an example to women everywhere, but she would also admit that it was worth it.

As we move ever farther into the twenty first century, we will see scenes like this one re-enacted in increasing numbers with each passing year. Now let's find out what I *REALLY* think about women in the twenty first century.

****

So far in this book, I have spent a lot of time talking about how women have progressed as people during the course of history and I have provided a lot of historical evidence to illustrate how difficult their struggles have been. I have talked about some of the difficulties that men have in communicating with women and why men don't always understand them. I have made it clear that much of the motivation that women and men have is unavoidably based in evolution and DNA, and I have passed along a lot of scientific information about hormonal and chemical reactions to all sorts of human stimuli. I have talked about heterosexuals, lesbians, and gorillas. Hopefully, I have passed along some useful relationship advice to men and women alike…but I have deliberately not made it clear how I feel personally about women in general. I was saving that for the last chapter and here it is…

Let me say firstly, *"I have not met a woman I did not like."* I have grown to dislike some of them over time but it is safe to say that I have not disliked any woman because of her womanhood and I dare say that I have disliked more men than women. I think if most normal men were to dig deep and exercise complete honesty, they would have to say the same. We have all run across women that we eventually did not like, but usually our revulsion or repulsion resulted from non-gender-related differences of opinion or behavioral transgressions that we could neither justify nor forgive. I can confidently say that almost every time I meet a woman, I feel comfortable and secure at first blush. A woman must work hard to destroy my faith in her and she will never damage my overall faith in the feminine gender no matter how hard she might try. I do not feel threatened by women, and in most cases, women seem to go out of their way to make my life better. I don't think my experience with women is unusual and I would suggest that any man who feels differently has deeply rooted issues with women that might be based in some sort of emotional or psychological upheaval during his early life. Simply put, normal guys enjoy the company of women and want to spend time with them.

I started this book with some historical references to famous, heroic women. When I wrote that chapter, I had in mind that there have been a number of women throughout the course of time that have set themselves apart by doing things that were not typical of their gender. In most cases, those women challenged the male dominated hierarchy of the world and made themselves famous for their good works. Had they not challenged the male leaders of their various eras, the good work they did would never have occurred and the world would not be the place it is today. That is what historically famous people do…they create history that lives on and shapes the culture of the world for all time. Clearly our world can be shaped by women just as it has been by men and I can't help but wonder what it would have looked like if even more feminine ideas had been allowed to flourish and impact on mother earth. We cannot change the past, but we can imagine what great things Joan of Arc might be able to do as a General in the American military today. Imagine Elizabeth Fry as a leader in today's world, going up against the current American Government for the rights of those less fortunate. Think about how a young Rosa Parks might have helped political leaders of the twenty first century as they struggle with the challenges of human rights. Ponder what the USA, and indeed the world, will look like when a woman becomes the President of the United States. Finally, give some consideration to how the lives of women in the twenty first century have been impacted upon and improved by powerful media spokeswomen and female politicians. The world is a much better place because of all of these women and I think it will continue to improve exponentially as more and more women take their rightful places in history. So how can we make it possible for every other woman on earth to take her rightful place in society?

From my male perspective, it appears to me that the famous ladies I mentioned earlier were single minded and oblivious to the apparent power of their male counterparts. They pursued their causes with determination and devotion. They probably experienced a great deal of trepidation and outright fear as they set out upon the pathways of their raisons d'être; but they forged on. They met the dragon of male chauvinism in his lair and they slew him. These women were all much better than me. They are also much better than almost every man on earth. They are exceptional, but that does not mean that every other woman cannot be exceptional in her own right. You don't need to have the heritage of Cleopatra or the tenacity of Susan B. Anthony in order to be a significant woman in today's world.

What most men look for in a woman today is intelligence and a nurturing nature. They want someone who can match or better them in a conversation and who will look after them. Yes, unfortunately, because of the male hunter-gatherer nature, they tend to be less tidy than women and they are major wimps when they are stricken with illness or injury. Women who are willing to clean up after men and make them chicken soup when they have a cold or flu instead of criticizing them or ignoring them will find their men much easier to get along with. I know some women would prefer that men did the lion's share of the cooking, cleaning, and nurturing, but most of us are simply not that evolved yet. I must admit that there are also, still some men who prefer their women to be dim, silent, and at the beck and call of their men at all times. However, I think it is safe to say that those guys are reducing in numbers with each passing year. Most of us will allow our woman to become a driving force in our life if she meets the basic parameters that we have for her. Fortunately, women are rising to the occasion and as our ever-more-indulgent world demands that we have more and more consumer products and creature comforts, income-producing women are garnering more respect and power in their relationships than ever before. Keep in mind however that a relationship where a woman actually earns more money than her man still runs the risk of the male hunter-gatherer ego rearing up and destroying it.

As a typical male, I have often felt, and continue to feel that women sometimes react to male actions, male commentary, and male attitudes with unfair disdain. It is evident to me that because of past indiscretions and poor behavior by some men, many women are harboring serious grudges that will probably take centuries to erase. Unfortunately, when women employ bad behavior and negative attitudes toward men due to past or current indiscretions, they tend to sharpen the knife of chauvinism and gender bias to a finely honed edge. Men are still hunter-gatherers and they will exercise their collective might to hold back, and keep down those women who choose not to live by their rules. That brings me back to the great women of history. How did they manage to force their way past the great wall of testosterone? How did they snub their noses at all of the men who wanted to hold them back and emerge victorious? How is it that some women are so much stronger than so many men while others seem so weak? The answer is clear to me. Those famous women were all blessed with three significant qualities: *intelligence, courage, and determination*. All were smart enough to do virtually anything they set their minds on; all were brave beyond belief; and all were tenacious and stubborn enough to *never give up*! The way powerful women become powerful is to set their minds on success and then summon up all of their willpower to finish what they set out to do. They do not accept failure as an option and they do not take *no* for an answer. They embodied the old adage of the United States Marine Corps, *Semper Fi* or *Semper Fidelis*. *Semper Fidelis* is Latin for *Always Faithful*. The great women of history managed to remain faithful to their respective causes despite the pressure brought to bear by the men who wanted to hold them back. If you look closely into the history of their successes, most of those powerful women were thoughtful, polite, and kind. They created their power with quiet feminine determination that was relentless and irresistible. Mother Teresa proved that quiet determination; unbelievable courage and unshakeable kindness in a woman can grant her the power to change the world. All of the great women of history refused to stop pushing ever forward toward their ultimate goals until they had *won*, and they proved to the men of their various eras that they were *right*. My advice to all women of the twenty first century is to always remain true to your own causes and philosophies, but do not fall into the trap of indicting men of unrelated ancient crimes or non-existent chauvinistic transgressions simply because they oppose you. More often than not, men make decisions that affect women negatively only because they don't like the situation at hand...not because they are chauvinists. If they are accused of chauvinism when none exists in their hearts, men will generally take it very personally and conclude that their integrity has been questioned. When that happens their testosterone-fueled ire will invariably begin to rise and all reason will take flight.

In business, Ladies I recommend that you do NOT mimic the actions of successful businessmen. Women who exhibit the overt dominance and unbending intolerance of men tend to come across badly. The world expects male business leaders to be hard and intimidating, but our society simply does not like to see those traits in women at any level of business. The powerful female business leaders I know command respect from all who meet them because they exude an air of calmness and femininity along with an aura of sophisticated elegance and intelligence. Rightly or wrongly, women who want to take a seat at the head of a boardroom table must be women first and captains of industry second. They must be talented and they must know their stuff. In fact they must know their business better than any man and they must be willing to express their knowledge of it passionately and confidently. If you are good at something or you know more about something than anyone else, let the world know about it! If you push fear away and stay true to yourself as

Rosa Parks and Joan of Arc did, you will emerge victorious. You don't need testosterone, big muscles, or a booming voice to get what you want…like all heroines throughout history, you just have to *try* to do whatever it is you have a passion for and keep on *trying* until the job is done.

Can you woo us with sexual attraction? Sure you can, but for most men, sex is just sex. If we like you because you are sexy or because you provide us with fabulous sexual encounters, our relationships will begin and end with sex. Women will not be successful due to sex alone unless they are in the business of sex…where, by the way, long-term romantic relationships are rare at best. Men love sex, but the staying power of any romantic relationship is based on the qualities of loyalty, intelligence, courage, steadfastness and most importantly, emotional love. A woman who grabs on to the heart and soul of her man with all of the strength she can muster stands a much better chance of hanging on to him for life than one who relies on sheer sexual attractiveness or bedroom gymnastics to make the grade. It might be acceptable in the twenty first century to attract a man with the promise of sex, but as the ever-growing North American divorce rate attests, marriage is tough and it will take a lot more than sex to keep it together. Remember Ladies: men can get sex almost anywhere, at almost any time these days so you need to have some other romantic arrows in your quiver. For me, a great brain and a good sense of humor are much more appealing and enduring than a great body and a short skirt, any day.

Are men *pigs*? In our twenty-first century politically correct world, I suppose we are. Men tend to feel a sexual urge whenever they are faced with anything resembling the sight, sound, smell or touch of a potential sexual encounter. Many women I know complain when men look at their breasts. That's a tough one, Ladies because your breasts are generally stuck out there for all to see. When men see them, testosterone kicks in and our imaginations take flight. We are drawn to breasts like a moth to a flame and if you emphasize them in any way, you can expect men to look at them. The same goes for butts, legs and crotches. We are lookers and we like to look at stuff that excites us. As long as there is human reproduction and coital sex, you can expect men to look at female body parts. It is neither abnormal nor unusual. It is simply one of the many facts of life, so you should probably get used to it. What is not acceptable however is overt staring, pointing, salacious commentary, or deliberate, unwanted touching. If that happens, for goodness sake, put a stop to it. We might be *pigs*, but we are not monsters and any man who deliberately goes out of his way to make our gender look bad should be put in his place.

In case you were wondering what the average man thinks about provocatively dressed women, I can tell you that the response varies amongst men and it depends on the situation at hand. When a man is in the presence of an attractive woman with a lot of exposed skin and *sexy* or *hot* attire he will generally be aroused, excited and intrigued. His testosterone will almost immediately overtake his common sense and he will have an overwhelming desire to stare and get closer to her. However if that same man is put into a position of dating that woman or even marrying her, at some point he will probably ask her to cover up and tone down her sexuality. There are two reasons for that. Firstly, men are generally jealous and possessive by nature and don't enjoy having other men ogling their women. Secondly, an overtly sexually appealing woman is often not considered a desirable mate and she is generally not someone a man wants to introduce to his mother. At worst she might be considered a harlot or a slut and at best, she might be merely a *trophy-date* or a *trophy-wife*. The man might want to show her off for a while but often the embarrassment of his obvious motives will get the better of him and he will drop her like a hot potato. Many men will avoid overtly sexy women altogether simply because being in the presence of them might bring unwanted and uncomfortable attention. The bottom line, Ladies is that what you consider a *sexy* appearance might be repelling more men than it is attracting!

The conundrum for women is that although an overtly sexy presentation might be a turn off for men in the long run, a dowdy, conservative appearance is even more unappealing. Boring, frumpy women have a great deal of difficulty attracting men because the comparative attractiveness of a man's mate is a matter of great pride for him. Every man visualizes himself with an outstandingly beautiful woman on his arm and despite his jealousy and possessiveness his ego gets a huge stroking when other men are attracted to her. Women, who start out in a relationship slim, well groomed, attractive, and sexy but allow their appearance to falter later in the relationship, run the risk of their man seeking out extra-marital affairs or even a divorce. The only solution I can offer to the challenge of aesthetic appearance is to think, "*conservatively-sexy.*" In other words always maintain a body fat index that gives the appearance of health (but not anorexia) and always wear clothing that is flatteringly feminine but not provocative. I am sure the fashion experts of the world can help with that.

I love women in the workplace. I am a firm believer that women are great workers. My experience is that rather than thinking only about advancement and greater income, they take great pride in doing the job at hand. Men tend to be constantly on the move and looking for promotions and raises. They often consider their current work to be just a means to a better end. It is a stepping-stone with lesser value than what they want to do in the future. To a man, the current moment's work is impermanent and therefore of less importance. Women on the other hand think of their work as the most important thing they can do at that moment in time and they will not visualize the future until the current work is done. That is not to say that they do not desire advancement, money, or status. It is only to say that they consider the attainment of those things as a separate effort that should be taken up only *after* the current work is complete. It is a fact that women multi-task better than men and due to their kind, nurturing nature they tend to create a less combative and more cooperative workplace.

Where possible, I prefer to see a balance of men and women in any workplace. Men tend to withhold some of their natural aggression when women are present and women tend to have fewer arguments with each other when men are present. Just as in a wolf pack, when one gender is forced to live and work together exclusively, tempers eventually flare and battles for dominance within the gender often break out. Men and women working together, side by side create a balanced, more natural and healthy environment where people can accomplish things. Both genders enjoy being complimented by the other and a workplace with men and women in it tends to create and maintain a bit of sexual tension that causes everyone to want to do well. Success is a sign of strength and power that is attractive to men and women alike and because of that, neither gender wants to let the other down. I would like to see more executive groups and corporate boards adopting this ideal for their teams as well. A top level executive group comprised of an equal number of men and women would, in many cases, develop better plans and make consistently better decisions. The union of the cautious optimism of females and the dramatic aggressiveness of males would stand a greater chance of creating an enviably wise and decisive decision making group. I hope we will see more fully integrated boards and executive groups in the not too distant future.

I genuinely enjoy being in the presence of *smart* women. When I use the word smart, I am not just talking about intelligence. Women who display great knowledge, talent, and an ability to get things done are a real turn on for me. Don't get me wrong...raw intelligence is good too and I find it very appealing. I think some men shy away from very intelligent women because it is difficult to be condescending or demeaning to someone who is smarter than oneself. And of course, very smart women are naturally better equipped to create larger income levels than average men and women. As mentioned earlier, the average man will feel inferior to a woman who bests him on the personal income front and therefore his fragile male ego will often prevent him from forming any sort of emotional bond with a smarter female. Personally, I get a real kick out of seeing a smart woman best a man in a technical argument or a battle of wits. I am also imperceptibly drawn to the aura and perhaps even the pheromones of intelligent ladies. I find myself wanting to spend great amounts of time with women who hold my interest on an intellectual level, while I quickly lose interest in even strikingly beautiful women who have little knowledge of the world or what goes on in it. To me it is tragic to find an intelligent woman doing a job that does not require any real intelligence or talent at all. I do however, come across that phenomenon surprisingly often. It seems that some women will accept lesser roles because they have bought-in to the theory of male dominance and female inferiority. Don't play dumb, Ladies! If you are smart, display your talents for the world to see and use them to build a better place for yourself in society. Don't let anyone hold you back!

I hope, by now you have recognized the fact that I have a genuine, healthy, and abiding respect for women. It is not an act and it is not for the purpose of selling books. It is a fact that I love women...I really do! I did a lot of research and spent a lot of time writing this book for the purpose of assisting both genders to understand each other a little bit better. I hope the words in this book will reduce or bring about a complete halt to some of the animosities and negative behaviors men and women invariably bring to relationships. I also have a secondary agenda that I will share with you now. Firstly, the most important challenges that all men and women must face are how we can establish ground rules, create mutually agreeable expectations, and bring equality to every male/female scenario on earth. If we could stop feeling badly about each other and stop thinking negative things about each other, we could probably come up with a universal plan for world peace or even end all pain and suffering on planet earth. Equal utilization of the gifts, skills, and ideas of every woman and man on earth is the secret to resolving all problems (man-made and otherwise) we have before us. I truly believe that because men and women have wasted so much time finding fault with each other the human race has lost thousands of years of progress. If you imagine how many millions of hours have been squandered on holding women back and protesting for women's rights, you will quickly grasp where I am coming from.

On a more grass roots level, in the workplaces of the world the constant buzz about fairness and equality has gobbled up millions of hours of working time. Talk, talk, talk about women's issues and male chauvinism has probably been responsible for the loss of trillions of dollars of collective corporate profit in North America alone. On a purely personal level, I have already wasted thousands of the approximately 750,000 hours that I expect to live, (assuming I survive to age 85) discussing male/

female issues and dealing with them. I cannot get those hours back but I hope that future generations can spend their time on more positive and progressive things. Let's face it, some of the things that men have subjected women to are just plain silly and some of the protests that I have heard about men from women are right up there on the silliness scale. It all has to stop! Come on, People, you know I am right!

If you enjoyed this book, I am happy and grateful. If you did not enjoy it, I understand. Our society is not yet completely comfortable with the idea of equality between men and women. It has become crystal clear to me that the competitive nature of human beings and our natural human ego are two of the main stumbling blocks to a world of truly peaceful relationships. If we were able to universally overcome those two human traits on a gender-specific basis, we could begin to move closer to a kinder, gentler world. I know some men reading my words will think I am a traitor to their cause, just as I know some women will think I am presumptuous and have no business writing about them at all. I hope the majority of my readers understand why I wrote this book, and accept that it is my small way of trying to make our planet a better place for us all.

Women are wonderful and they should be celebrated. As I push the SAVE button and end my writing, I am raising a glass to you, Ladies. You are the best!

The end for me. A new beginning for you!

Wayne Kehl
www.waynekehl.com